Brian Fleming
Ministry of Education
Ministry of Training, Colleges & Universities
900 Bay St. 13th Floor, Mowat Block
Toronto, ON M7A 1L2

THE Boiling Frog Dilemma

THE Boiling Frog Dilemma

SAVING CANADA
FROM ECONOMIC DECLINE

Todd Hirsch & Robert Roach

© 2012 Todd Hirsch & Robert Roach

All rights reserved. The use of any part of this publication, reproduced, transmitted in any form or by any means, electronic, mechanical, photocopying, recording, or otherwise, or stored in a retrieval system, without written consent of the authors, is an infringement of copyright law.

ISBN 978-0-9879269-0-6

P & P Publishing
713, 3249 66 Avenue SW
Calgary, AB T3E 6M5
robroach@shaw.ca

For information about *The Boiling Frog Dilemma*, visit: **www.toddhirsch.com**

Printed and bound in Canada by McCallum Printing Group Inc.

Graphic Design by Sophie Lacerte

Contents

VII Foreword by Dr. Roger Gibbins

IX Preface

XI Acknowledgements

01 Introduction

13 PART A: The Problem – Is it Getting Hot in Here?

15 Chapter 1: Canadian Manufacturing in Transition

25 Chapter 2: Natural Resources in the 21st Century

29 Chapter 3: The Tightly-Knit Global Economy

37 Chapter 4: Flying Under the Radar

53 Chapter 5: How Do I Look? Why Profile Matters in the International Economy

59 Epilogue to Part A

63 PART B: The Solution – A New Economic DNA for Canada

65 Chapter 6: Unleashing Creativity

85 Chapter 7: More Than Tourists – Developing a More Cosmopolitan Economy

101 Chapter 8: Moving Up the Value Chain

115 Chapter 9: Embracing Risk and Accepting Failure

129 Chapter 10: Green is the New Black

143 Chapter 11: The Social Gene

155 Chapter 12: The New Canadian Entrepreneur

171 Conclusion: No Frog Legs Please

174 Endnotes

178 Bibliography

183 Author Biographies

For Jason, Jax & Xander
(and Puma, Pixie & Penny, too).

Foreword

The spark of creativity often comes when optimism collides with frustration, when writers can see, almost taste and touch, a better future but find themselves mired in a status quo world of conventional thinking. As I read Todd Hirsch and Robert Roach's prescription for curing the ills that threaten the future vitality of the Canadian economy, I was struck by their belief that we can do better coupled with frustration that Canadians are slow to recognize the challenges we face much less embrace creative solutions.

Somewhat paradoxically, *The Boiling Frog Dilemma* is both familiar and new. My familiarity with the themes stems from my job at the Canada West Foundation—a job that has given me the opportunity to meet with countless community leaders, policymakers, business people and other Canadians interested in ensuring Canada's long-term economic prosperity. In one way or another, elements of the challenges facing the Canadian economy and the potential solutions outlined in *The Boiling Frog Dilemma* have come up again and again at these meetings. Canada needs to do more to attract the world's best and brightest. Innovation is key. Canada needs to reach out to new international markets. Canadians have to get better at environmental stewardship. Risks bring rewards. A good society is the basis of a strong economy. Resources are critical but so is the creative economy.

Hirsch and Roach have collected these strands and woven them into a coherent and convincing argument for how Canadians can ensure a bright economic future for themselves. Having everything pulled together in one place in such a powerful way was new even though reading each chapter was like hanging out with an old friend.

What sets *The Boiling Frog Dilemma* apart is the sense of urgency that the authors bring to their analysis. They argue, and I would agree, that sustained economic prosperity is not a birthright, but something that has to be earned day in and day out in an increasingly competitive global economy.

Their vision of a new and more competitive economy is not the only one possible, but this book is essential reading for everyone who has experienced the nagging feeling that Canadians have some hard work to do if we are to remain a prosperous nation. To this end, Hirsch and Roach offer optimism and a way forward, both of which are badly needed in a time of economic uncertainty.

Dr. Roger Gibbins, President and CEO, Canada West Foundation

Preface

When the two of us began thinking about this book back in 2007, the global economy was in pretty good shape. The North America economy was zipping along, the US housing market was hitting records and just about everything the Canadian economy touched was turning to gold.

But when we starting writing, the Great Recession of 2009 was in full swing. We were a bit worried that a book about maximizing creativity, embracing failure, and becoming more cosmopolitan would fall on deaf ears amid the shock and awe of all the bad financial news. And now, as we approach completion of the book near the end of 2011, America's credit rating has been downgraded, and a double-dip recession is a distinct possibility. Global equity markets are very unstable, governments in Europe are teetering on the brink of bankruptcy, and the Canadian economy is bracing itself as the global headwinds bear down.

Yet rather than coming too late, we believe that *The Boiling Frog Dilemma* comes at just the right time. Despite the ups and downs—indeed, *because of the ups and downs*—the way forward we outline is worth considering. The notion that only ideas can create wealth and prosperity is more compelling than ever.

The metaphor of the boiling frog dates back to experiments performed in the 1800s. According to some accounts, a frog dropped into a pot of hot water will scramble furiously to escape, thus saving itself. But a frog placed in a pot of cool water that is heated very gradually will fail to recognize the danger. The frog's body adjusts to the rising temperature, but at a certain point it is too late and the frog—in its complacency—boils to death. (Some modern experiments have shown, in fact, that a frog will indeed jump out of the water when it reaches an uncomfortable temperature. Nonetheless, as a metaphor for the dangers of complacency and unwillingness to act, the boiling frog story is disturbingly instructive.)

This book argues that Canada's economy is much like a frog in a pot of water that is gradually being heated. As a nation, we face a pressing dilemma. One choice is to stay put and be boiled to death. The other is to make some difficult but necessary changes to how we think about Canada's economy, take a leap of faith, and jump out of the pot! Neither option is appealing—but only the second one is acceptable.

The global economy's current troubles do not challenge the premise that Canada's economy needs to adapt. If anything, they highlight the need for a more resilient ideas-driven economy.

A second key thing to note is that we don't claim to have the *only* map to a prosperous economic future for Canada. We offer our recipe for change in the spirit of sparking discussion. Many will disagree and offer alternatives. *That's* the debate.

Todd Hirsch & Robert Roach
Calgary
December 2011

Acknowledgements

First and foremost, we want to acknowledge our parents—Ken and Rita Hirsch, and Boyd and Betty Roach—for all the love and support they have provided over the years.

Many people have helped us with this project in many different ways. We are especially thankful to our friends and families for putting up with us and for listening patiently to our half-formed thoughts. In early 2009, we pulled together a group of thoughtful people and asked them to give us feedback on our main themes. We are grateful to each of them: Jennifer Allford, Paula Arab, Jan Eden, Clark Grue, John Gulak, Cathy Hodgson, Janet Lane, John Larsen, Kevin Peterson, Julie Pithers, Karin Põldaas, Terry Rock, Bruce Sellery, Shelley Uytterhagen, Karen Wilkie and Michael Willmott. We also imposed upon a number of people to read a draft and we are thankful for their feedback: Jennifer Allford, Loleen Berdahl, Jock Finlayson, Adam Legge, Jacques Marcil, Kari Roberts, Ian Wild and Karen Wilkie. Responsibility for any errors, omissions or nutty ideas remains entirely ours.

We also want to thank the many people who we interviewed and pestered for information and insight. We are grateful for the time and thoughts that you shared with us.

Todd is very grateful to his employer, ATB Financial, for providing a sabbatical leave. Todd also extends special thanks to Julie Braaten, Bart Doan and Catriona Le May Doan, and Joe and Norma Sebestyen for use of their residences in Kelowna, Invermere, and Vancouver, British Columbia, respectively. Without their generous support, the book may not have happened.

We are especially indebted to all the creative people who have inspired us and to the many authors whose ideas we have so freely plundered.

Note: No frogs were harmed, boiled, or even slightly inconvenienced in the preparation of this book.

Introduction

> "There may be a limit to the number of good factory jobs in the world, but there is no limit to the number of idea-generated jobs in the world."
> —Thomas Friedman, The World is Flat: A Brief History of the Twenty-First Century

> Apparently, if you put a frog in a pot of water and *slowly* turn up the heat, it will not realize what it happening until it is too late.
> —Anonymous

Canada the Invisible

The *Pocket World in Figures 2011* is a handy little publication from the publishers of *The Economist* magazine. It's a page-turner for those who love lists of country rankings. But for any Canadian flipping through the book, an uncomfortable truth quickly becomes apparent: Canada doesn't seem to exist. Often the rankings are for the superlatives—only the highest or lowest among the nations—and Canada is missing from almost all of them.

Canada is like the guy who gets his picture in the newspaper standing among a group of celebrities or politicians. He's in the back row and half his head is cropped out of the shot. His misspelled name appears in the line that starts "Also pictured are... ." No one notices the mistake, and no one cares.

Consider Canada's presence on lists of economic achievement. Highest economic growth? Nope. Largest services output as a percent of its economy? Hardly. Largest companies? Forget it. Not even in the top fifty. Yes, Canada is a smallish country. But how do we explain much smaller countries on these lists, like Australia, the Netherlands, Denmark and Finland?

Canada ranks only 15th in spending on research and development (as a percentage of GDP), 15th in patents and a sickly 17th on an index of IT technology.

In a world of 101 flavours of ice cream, Canada is vanilla: reliable, but boring.

At stake is much more than bragging rights that come with higher rankings on these lists; the future prosperity of Canada is in jeopardy. The global economy is changing so rapidly that Canada can no longer prosper simply by being the bland, invisible, and increasingly irrelevant country that it is. There is far too much potential and talent in this country that is being wasted chasing old industries and old ways of doing things.

In labs, cafes and boardrooms around the world, people need to be saying things like "we need the Canadians involved," "I want to study in Canada" and "Canada has exactly what we need." Popping up now and then on the international radar screen is not good enough. Canada needs to be a ubiquitous presence in the international economy.

If the Canadian economy is going to survive and thrive in the global economic environment, it needs to become an entirely new economic animal. Canadians need to capitalize on their potential for creativity, become more outward looking, get more comfortable with risk, become more resilient in the face of failure, grow stronger socially and environmentally, and compete with the best of the best at the top of the global economic food chain.

Forget plain old vanilla. Canada can do better.

Evolve or Die

This book is about the future of Canada. Not the distant future, but the near future. It's about a future in which Canada is a prosperous place in which "good" (i.e., interesting, lucrative and long-lasting) jobs are available to as many Canadians as possible.

Small adjustments will not get the job done. The Canadian economy needs to be altered in a number of *fundamental* ways. The metaphor we use to express this is drawn from evolutionary theory: organisms that cannot adapt to new conditions go extinct. Those that mutate in ways that give them an edge, survive and, with a bit of luck, thrive.

The global economy has changed, and it will continue to change rapidly in the coming years. If Canadians don't adjust, their current prosperity could well go "extinct." This will not be as dramatic as the disappearance of the dinosaurs, but it will mean a major drop in Canada's standard of living over time and the erosion of the good things that standard of living makes possible. If Canadians sit still, Canada could go from being a member of the G8 with one of the highest standards of living in the world to a bit player on the global stage, struggling desperately to return to the good old days of economic prosperity.

A key difference between the Canadian economy and a living organism—a ground hog, say, or an amoeba—is that Canadians don't have to wait for generations of genetic mutations to take place in order to evolve. Rather, Canadians can *proactively* alter their country's economic DNA; new bits of genetic code can be inserted that will transform Canada into a wealth generating powerhouse that is able to compete and win in the global competition for good jobs.

The alternative is to stick to our knitting, resist adapting, and stubbornly refuse to change our attitudes. This book argues that Canadians don't have this luxury. The world is changing. Canadians will either change with it or fall permanently behind in the global quest for ongoing economic prosperity.

Part of the problem is that Canada's economic demise, like the frog in a pot of water with the temperature slowly rising, is not immediately obvious. The Canadian economy can probably bumble along as it has for many more years before major drops in Canada's standard of living are observed. This breeds complacency that Canadians can't afford.

The Boiling Frog Dilemma highlights the critical strands of code that need to be inserted into Canada's existing economic DNA. It's intended to inspire Canadians and Canadian businesses and to encourage them to alter their attitudes and priorities as a means of making the Canadian economy more competitive. Whether it is transforming Canada's education system so as to unleash the creativity innate in all of us or cultivating a new form of international entrepreneurialism, the changes have to come from the ground up, not the top down—they have to come from individual action, not government programs.

A Faster Horse?

A quotation attributed to Henry Ford sums up the challenge: "If I had asked people what they wanted, they would have said a faster horse." When it comes to Canada's economic DNA—the core attributes that shape how the economy operates—it needs to change from a horse to a Lamborghini. Canadians need to be ready to capture the good jobs that *haven't even been thought of yet*.

None of this denies the fact that Canada has enjoyed a good run. Prime Minister Laurier said that the 20th century would belong to Canada, and he was right. Canada went from a backwater British colony to a global economic power (not to mention liberator of occupied countries and international peacekeeper). With only 34 million people, Canada is the 11th largest economy in the world, the 11th largest exporter and a magnet for tens of thousands of skilled immigrants every year.[1] Canadians have special access to the world's largest economy. Canada's economic power has enabled it to offer one of the highest standards of living in the world.

Can this be sustained?

Canada's success so far has depended on two fundamental economic drivers: natural resources and manufacturing. These are the economic pillars upon which Canada's modern service economy and social safety net were built.

Canadians started out selling beaver pelts and now they sell oil, gas, uranium, electricity, potash, nickel, trees, beef, wheat, canola and a long list of other natural resources. At the same time, Canadians worked hard and developed an impressive amount of industrial manufacturing capacity. Through savvy deals with US partners, Canada morphed into a major auto sector manufacturer. Notwithstanding the ups and downs of the business cycle and global shocks, Canada has done well.

But the world has changed. You don't need a PhD in economics to see that globalization has run roughshod over the old regime. People lament that "we don't *make* things in Canada anymore." This is because many of the things Canadians used to manufacture can be made more cheaply somewhere else. When we were kids, we had lots of toys that said "Made in Canada." Today, toys come from China or somewhere else that has a ready supply of relatively cheap labour. There is still manufacturing in Canada, and there will be for the foreseeable future, but old school manufacturing is not going to be the economic driver it once was.

This is good news because Canadians don't *want* to be competing at the bottom end of the global value chain making stuff that ends up in dollar stores. As described in Chapter 8, the real action and the good jobs are at the *top* of the international value chain; Canada is ideally suited to occupying this position.

The story for natural resources is a little different, but concludes in roughly the same way. Canada is full to the brim with natural resources that the world needs. The US has been buying raw and semi-raw resources from Canada for a long time and the rise of resource-hungry new powerhouses like China has the potential to open lucrative new markets for Canadian resource exporters (assuming Canada can put in place the infrastructure needed to transport more of its resources to Asia).

Commodity markets are notoriously volatile (and for this reason alone, not the best basis upon which to build a stable and prosperous economy), but you put up with the busts because of the booms. One province in particular—Alberta—embodies the boom-and-bust economic cycle. But booms and busts are not limited to Alberta. Dozens of cities, towns and regions across Canada live through the ups-and-downs of commodity cycles and some have seen their keystone industry leave never to come back. Fortunately, the booms have been frequent enough (and the busts brief enough) that, overall, Canada has had a pretty good ride on the commodities rollercoaster.

However, at least two things threaten the future of commodity booms in Canada and make the busts more worrisome. First, just as in manufacturing, the forces of globalization[2] are also at work in the natural resource sector in the form of foreign competitors aggressively seeking to capture market share. For example, Canada has lots of trees, but other countries with ample trees are getting better and better at the forestry products game. Keeping up with technological change, competing against jurisdictions with lower labour costs, developing better forest management techniques and shifting trading relationships have made forestry a much tougher business than it once was. It's not enough to just have a lot of trees. This doesn't mean that Canadians can't compete in this and other resource sectors, but it does mean that their slice of the international commodities pie could shrink as competitors utilize their growing comparative advantages.

The second threat is the increasingly widespread desire to mothball fossil fuels in favour of greener options. Some want to see this happen to address climate change, some are in favour because they are sick of smog and oil spills, some want to increase energy security and some see lucrative opportunities in supplying alternative energy. This is problematic because Canada's biggest natural resource export is fossil fuel and its most important customer—the United States—is thinking hard about how to wean itself off the stuff. It has not done much yet, but if it does, this would throw a big wrench into what has become a primary economic engine for Canada (witness the opposition to the proposed Keystone XL pipeline that would carry oil sands oil to the US).

Canada may be able to find other customers, but China and other energy-hungry countries might move even faster than the US. If electric cars and trucks that run on natural gas take off the way some hope they will, Canada's oil sector may feel the pinch. The commodity booms that make the whole thing worthwhile may become a thing of the past. Even if this doesn't happen, or takes decades to come to fruition, prudence demands that Canadians prepare for the worst rather than just hope for the best.

As with traditional manufacturing, the natural resource sector in Canada—including the oil patch—is not going to disappear, but it will be subject to some dramatic change due to international competition, environmental concerns and new technology. More importantly, selling natural resources *is not enough on its own* to keep the Canadian economy growing at the rate to which Canadians have become accustom. The oil sands can help drive the Canadian economy, but it can't do it alone.

So if traditional manufacturing and natural resources have brought Canada this far, but may not be able to keep the economy going in the decades ahead, what can Canadians do to find new economic drivers?

The Solution

The first point to stress is that Canadians have to do more than fiddle at the margins of how the economy operates. Hence, the DNA metaphor: Canada needs change at a *fundamental* level that ripples out into every nook and cranny of its economy. The goal is not only an economic revolution, but a social one as well. Canadians need to break old habits, think differently and see the world in new ways for this to work. One-offs, band-aids and half-baked efforts will probably do more harm than good and they will certainly fall short of what is needed.

The second key point is that Canadians can't rely on government to get the job done—individuals, families, entrepreneurs, businesses, investors, educators, community leaders and nonprofit organizations need to lead the transformation with government coming along for the ride. There are some very important things that government needs to do and there are lots of reports outlining policy suggestions for governments. This book, therefore, is focused on Canadians rather than their governments.

The third point is that the ideas presented here will not generate the degree of transformation needed if Canadians cherry-pick from them; they are a *package* deal with each element reinforcing the others. When we say we need to emphasize creativity in Canada's schools and workplaces, embrace risk, become a more cosmopolitan society, focus on the top-end of the value chain, cultivate a new breed of entrepreneur, fully integrate green processes and expand social capital, we are referring to parts of a system rather than stand-alone themes to be independently pursued.

For those who are tempted to toss this book away because the wholesale transformation of how the Canadian economy operates sounds either insane or impossible, take solace in the knowledge that not everything has to change. Think of the similarities and differences shared by humans and chimpanzees. Only a small percentage of human DNA is different from that of a chimp. But the parts that are different are very important. The same is true when it comes to altering Canada's economic DNA; changing a specific set of key things will be enough to enable an evolutionary leap forward. The result will be an economy able to adapt to a tougher international economic environment. Canada won't be stuck like the frog in the pot of boiling water because it will have jumped out and found ways to thrive in its new environment.

This book pulls together six core ideas for improving economic performance. These ideas have been examined by many brilliant thinkers. What we do is pull them together into a single plan for rewriting Canada's economic DNA.

1) Unbounded Creativity

Canadians are a creative people. They make great music. They discovered insulin. They figured out how to squeeze a commercial petroleum product from tarry sand. They gave the world John Candy and Arcade Fire. They made email truly portable via the Blackberry. The list goes on. This creativity has served Canadians well as they have carved out niches in the global economy and overcome the barriers that could have easily left Canada a much less prosperous nation.

Chapter 6 argues that creative brainpower will keep Canada's economy successful over the long haul rather than natural resources or industrial output. The more Canadians can think up things rather than actually making them or extracting them, the better off they will be. It is the creative sectors that will supply most of the good jobs. At the same time, getting more creative *in all sectors of the economy*—from mining and manufacturing to health care and tourism—will increase Canada's competitiveness and prosperity. The goal is to have a creative economy, not just a few creative sectors. Canadians have gone part way down this path, but they need to go from a walking pace to an all out sprint if they are to stay ahead of their competitors and generate enough creative output to truly drive the economy.

US President Barack Obama has stressed the importance of innovation to the US Economy:

> The first step in winning the future is encouraging American innovation. None of us can predict with certainty what the next big industry will be or where the new jobs will come from. Thirty years ago, we couldn't know that something called the Internet would lead to an economic revolution. What we can do—what America does better than anyone else—is spark the creativity and imagination of our people. We're the nation that put cars in driveways and computers in offices; the nation of Edison and the Wright brothers; of Google and Facebook. In America, innovation doesn't just change our lives. It is how we make our living.[3]

The same holds true for Canada. The challenge is to, if not out do the Americans, the Russians, the Chinese and every other country that is looking to take this route to economic success, then to at least be among the pack that is leading the race.

2) A Cosmopolitan Spirit

Chapter 7 explains why it is important for Canadians to be more outward looking. Canada is a wonderfully diverse society and this enriches both its culture and its economic prowess. Immigrants bring a different way of seeing things and of solving problems. They also bring international awareness and ties that grease the wheels of trade. When Canadians return home from trips to other countries, they bring back experiences and knowledge along with the jetlag and trinkets. Canada is a trading nation.

All of this points to a strong base of cosmopolitanism. As with the other ideas for change, the Canadian economy already shows strong signs of being an outward looking economic creature. The next step is to fully actualize this tendency. Canadians need to become more than just tourists in the global economy and they need to do more than just schlep their wares to foreign customers. Canada needs to become the world's business partner, its education centre, its source of creative ideas and knowledge services and an indispensible part of the international economy.

3) Occupying Top Spot on the Global Economic Food Chain

The global economic food chain offers many spots where Canada can locate itself. The last place Canada wants to be is at the bottom supplying cheap labour. Canadians have done well avoiding this fate. As China continues to grow its economy, it is becoming less and less satisfied with its cheap labour niche and is poised to move several links up the chain into the higher-end manufacturing that sustained the central Canadian economy for decades. This threat is just one of the reasons why Canada should be looking to vacate this spot and move further up the value chain.

Selling commodities has kept Canada further down the chain than it could be (hence the ongoing push to add more value to Canada's commodities before exporting them), but this has nonetheless been a source of wealth and well-paying jobs. As noted already, however, this is a volatile position in the value chain that makes it a questionable spot on which to base Canada's future economic prosperity. Canada can and should hang out here and see what comes along, but the bigger prize is still the top of the food chain where the world's designers, educators, managers and investors feast. This quest is discussed in Chapter 8.

4) Fearlessness

In her book *Why Mexicans Don't Drink Molson,* Andrea Mandel-Campbell accuses Canadian businesses of being wimps that are too timid to take full advantage of the many opportunities presented to them by the global economy. This is why Canadians drink buckets of Corona but Mexicans don't suck back six-packs of Molson.

As the saying goes, if you want big rewards, you gotta take big risks. It's a bit cliché (okay, a lot cliché), but that makes it no less true. Whether it is being bolder in international business dealings, accepting that failure is part of the creative and commercialization process or being willing to try new approaches to old problems, Canada's economic future will be brighter if Canadians are more fearless rather than less. Chapter 9 outlines why embracing more risk is so important to Canada's economic future.

5) Green Blood

Most would agree that the planet needs a little TLC. Whether it is disappearing fish stocks, smog, toxic waste in lakes and rivers or destruction of beautiful places, Canadians know that they can do better and that they need to tread more lightly on the earth. Increasingly, they are discovering (or rediscovering as the case may be) the tremendous value of the ecological goods and services that nature provides and upon which humans rely to survive such as clean water, productive soil and the soul-reviving aesthetic beauty of nature. Screwing this up is a bad idea that will cost Canadians in all sorts of ways that environmentalists and full-cost accounting economists rightly point out.

As a result, there are lots of reasons to be "green." Carefully considering the environment is part of doing business in Canada and, more and more, in the global economy. However, the wealth creation and good job-generating benefits of thinking green are still not fully evident and, in turn, not fully integrated into Canada's economic DNA. Canadians still tend to see the economy and the environment as competing forces locked in a zero-sum game. To some degree, this is true as economic activity inevitably disturbs the natural environment. But if you accept that it is not (literally) the end of the world if humans muck about a bit with their home, there are ways to reconcile getting ahead economically and keeping the environment healthy.

In fact, there are ways to not just reconcile environmental and economic goals, but to improve outcomes on both fronts. The economies that do this will have an edge over their competition in four ways. First, there are efficiency gains to be had by being less wasteful. Second, as consumers and regulators demand greener products, business that can meet these requirements will have an advantage. Third, there are opportunities to be the supplier of new green products and services. Fourth, maintaining, or even better, increasing natural capital avoids the costs associated with a degraded environment such as increased health care costs and repairing damaged ecological infrastructure. The key here is to make green behaviour an ingrained trait rather than an add-on, afterthought or burden. The value of having green economic blood is explored in Chapter 10.

6) Rubbing Ideas Together

Economic activity is an extension of social activity. Hence, a diverse, fair, friendly and peaceful society is better for an economy than a repressed, unjust, isolating and violent society. In the short-term, dictatorships can grow an economy through force, but the underlying social landmines will eventually go off and derail things. The rule of law, a relative lack of corruption, general prosperity (notwithstanding the gap between rich and poor), guaranteed rights and freedoms, relatively low crime rates and peaceful relations internally and with its neighbour all give Canada a huge economic advantage.

Writers such as Francis Fukuyama have highlighted the economic importance of social capital.[4] The more people interact with each other, understand each other and trust each other, the more likely they are to successfully work together on economic projects. If you think your neighbour is going to rip you off, you are unlikely to start a risky business venture with her. Similarly, because government plays such a large role in the economy through everything from taxes and regulations to business subsidies and publically-owned corporations, a lack of trust or satisfaction with political institutions is detrimental to economic competitiveness and growth. You have to trust not only your neighbour, but the folks running the government as well.

In addition, creativity, innovation and new ventures require people to share ideas, enthusiasm and capital. Canadians need to be running into each other, spending time together and working side by side. The lonely inventor in his basement is not a good model for economic growth. Collaboration is critical.

Fortunately, Canada has a plentiful supply of social capital. But, Canadians need to make sure that it gets even stronger in order to cultivate the interaction, familiarity, trust, collaboration and effective government needed to take more risks, translate creativity into commercial ventures and be a leading player on the world stage. This topic is explored in Chapter 11.

Putting it All Together: The New Canadian Entrepreneur

Canada has a lot of entrepreneurs, but they are still the exception rather than the rule. A new breed of entrepreneur who exemplifies the creative mind, who is adept at collaborating with people all over the world, who is willing to take big risks, who wants to be at the top of the global value chain, who bleeds green and who is a social butterfly and solid citizen is what will ensure a bright economic future for Canada. These entrepreneurs may be self-employed or they may find themselves working for giant companies. What links them together is a global outlook, a penchant for innovation, adherence to civic duty and a restlessness that rejects complacency and the idea that "good enough" is truly good. The businesses that harness these entrepreneurs and the investors who support them will thrive. Chapter 12 describes the ten key traits of the new Canadian entrepreneur.

An Attitude Adjustment

As mentioned earlier, this book is not about government policy (although this is one piece of the larger puzzle); it is about a *fundamental change in attitude*. Canadians often look to government to ensure their economic success despite the fact that governments are ill-equipped to play this role. Good public policy can facilitate economic growth (just as bad policy can hamper it), but no amount of government is a substitute for the wealth-generating actions taken by Canadian entrepreneurs and businesses. Canadians must rely on themselves as workers, investors, managers, parents, volunteers, neighbours, citizens and creative people.

At a presentation based on the ideas in this book, an audience member asked a key question: "How, exactly, do you make all this happen?" The *how* lies in convincing Canadians to see the value of, for example, living overseas for an extended period, unleashing their creativity, embracing risk and accepting that failure is part of the process. The *how* happens when parents encourage their kids to go work abroad for a year, when school boards and teachers reform the education system with an eye to building in a lot more creativity or when an investor says "I'll support that, even though it's risky." We provide the basic instructions, but it is up to individuals to put them into practice and give them life.

Unfortunately, many people are against innovative approaches because they are unfamiliar, risky or a threat to vested interests. People *want* to stick to their knitting because creativity and change scare them. Canada's current economic DNA is constantly whispering in the collective ear not to stray too far from home. In economic development meetings we've attended around the country, we constantly speak of the importance of creativity, innovation and embracing change. But invariably, someone puts up their hand and quips "these new ideas about creativity and such are all well and good, but let's not forget that oil (or auto parts, or chicken slaughterhouses—it varies by region) are our bread and butter." In other words, let's just stick with what has worked in the past.

If this fearful attitude is allowed to carry the day, it will scuttle the Canadian economy in the years ahead. Canadians need to aim much, much higher and rewrite the country's economic DNA or they will find themselves stuck in a pot of boiling water with no exit strategy.

Part A

The Problem → Is it Getting Hot in Here?

Chapter 1

Canadian Manufacturing in Transition

"Toto, I've a feeling we're not in Kansas any more."
—Dorothy in The Wizard of Oz

"If companies are operating the same way today as they did five years ago, they are likely in trouble (if they still exist); if they intend to operate the same way in five years time as they do today, they will likely be out of business."
—Jayson Myers, Canadian Manufacturers and Exporters

The Rise of Canada's Industrial Heartland

Canada has a long and complicated history with manufacturing as an engine of economic growth. Prior to Confederation in 1867, Nova Scotia was a respectable centre for shipbuilding, an activity that propelled the small British colony into considerable wealth. But in the years following Confederation, largely a result of the National Policy and other actions that favoured central Canada as a manufacturing hub, Nova Scotia's industrial might (and wealth) faded.

As the 20th century got underway, central Canada started to flex its manufacturing muscles and quickly grew into one of the world's most advanced manufacturing regions. Much of this, of course, was due to Canada's geographic proximity to the United States (a theme that repeats itself over and over again in Canadian history). Trade between Canada and the US blossomed and much of it was in heavy manufacturing.

In the years following the Second World War, Canada's industrial power grew stronger yet; by the mid-1960s, the Auto Pact with the US solidified Canada's position as a mass manufacturing power. In modern terminology, Canada had developed a heavy manufacturing "cluster." The corridor between Windsor and Quebec City became a formidable industrial power. Good paying jobs in auto assembly and the related parts manufacturing sector flourished, raising wages and standards of living. Ontario's Golden Horseshoe settled into its role as the centre of Canada's economy.

But a not-so-funny thing happened on the way to the 1970s: North America's car manufacturing prowess was challenged. Japan had the first go at it with its version of low-cost, low-quality cars. Initially met with laughs by American car companies, the likes of Toyota, Honda and Datsun (now Nissan) gradually grew into powerful competitors. By the early 1980s, Detroit and southern Ontario auto manufacturing was like a deer caught in headlights. The cracks in North America's manufacturing fortress were showing. The temperature of the water in the pot was on the rise.

Despite some reprieve in the 1990s, US automakers were in trouble again by the mid-2000s. The credit meltdown of 2008 pushed General Motors and Chrysler—two of the legends of American manufacturing—into bankruptcy and massive restructuring. If not for the lifelines thrown by US and Canadian governments, they'd be gone today.

Other manufacturing sectors in Canada—textiles, farm equipment, steel, food processing—have also seen better days. It's not that these (or car assembly for that matter) have vanished from the Canadian economy, and indeed some manufacturing companies continue to do very well. But most would agree that the golden days of traditional forms of manufacturing in Canada are behind us, just as they are in the United States.

The problem in all of this lies not in any specific mistakes made by North American mass manufactures. The problem is that emerging economies such as China, India, South Korea and Taiwan can do it much more cheaply (for which consumers are thankful). The shifting sands in manufacturing due to globalized trade are well documented. The bad news? American and Canadian manufacturers are simply no longer as competitive in many areas of mass production.

Adding to the dilemma for manufacturing is a higher valued Canadian dollar. For the 1980s, 1990s and the early years of the 2000s, a low-priced loonie gave a huge advantage to Canadian manufacturers and exporters. Some called it a crutch. Whatever you called it, though, it's gone. Since around 2005, the strength of the Canadian dollar (and weakness of the US dollar) has made it much more challenging for Canadian producers and exporters. It's impossible to predict with certainty the direction of the loonie in the years to come, but most economists predict that it will stay reasonably high, probably close to or above parity with the US greenback.

The significance of this current dilemma is felt most urgently in central Canada—the manufacturing powerhouse of the country. In a famous and somewhat controversial 2009 report entitled *Ontario in the Creative Age*, Roger Martin, Dean of the University of Toronto's Rotman School of Management, and his colleague Richard Florida, recommended ways of keeping Ontario competitive and prosperous:

> Our economy is shifting away from jobs based largely on physical skills or repetitive tasks to ones that require analytical skills and judgment.

This shift is also evident in the long-term trend away from employment in goods-producing to service industries, from occupations that depended on physical work to produce goods to ones that provide service and rely on creativity. The change is inexorable. We cannot turn away from it; nor can we slow it. The clock of history is always ticking. Competitive advantage and prosperity will go to those jurisdictions that can best prepare themselves and adapt to this long-run trend. We must embrace it and act in ways that create a distinctive advantage for the province and ensure our long-term prosperity.[5]

The report, which was commissioned by the Ontario provincial government and cost over $2.2 million, was not particularly well-received. *Maclean's* magazine, for example, dubbed the report "a map with no roads."[6] Still, the report highlighted the fact that Ontario's economy risked falling behind and becoming economically irrelevant if it did not take some intentional steps to correct its downward course.

Is There Really a Problem?

Manufacturers in Canada know that all is not well. And if comments by the head of the industry organization that represents manufacturers in the country are representative, they know that they're going to have to evolve to keep up with the changing global environment. "Probably the biggest challenge that Canadian manufacturers face is not getting product out the door, but providing customers with a special solution that few if any competitor can match," says Jayson Myers, President and CEO of the Canadian Manufacturers and Exporters. "In that sense, it's really a challenge of business leadership—how to restructure your business to succeed in new markets, with new products, using new technologies and processes, and utilizing the potential of your workforce."

Notice the heavy emphasis on the word *new*. Manufacturers in Canada are well aware that the world is changing around them and that enormous challenges lie ahead. "There are challenges that arise as a result of changing customer requirements, the loss of customer demand during the global recession, corporate consolidation and the re-organization of supply chains to which Canadian manufacturers must respond. There are the challenges and opportunities of structural changes in the global and Canadian economies—the shift of market growth away from developed economies, the implications of an aging population, the emergence of transformative technologies and growing environmental concerns," says Myers. "Business as usual is no longer an option."[7]

Despite the overwhelming evidence, the anecdotes, the reports from the management gurus and basic common sense, there will always be those who challenge the whole idea that Canadian manufacturers are in trouble. There are also those who accept that there is a problem, but argue that it is easily fixed by somehow reversing the forces of globalization. These voices can be loosely grouped into three schools of thought:

The Deniers: Some flat-out deny that Canadian manufacturing is facing any challenges whatsoever and that Canadians needn't fuss or worry because things are actually getting better. But all you have to do is look at the "made in" labels on the products you buy to know that traditional manufacturing in Canada has experienced a sea change.

The deniers are the classic frog in the pot that has somehow managed to trick itself into believing that the hotter water is really rather comfortable.

The Blamers: Others will admit that there are worrying challenges facing Canadian manufacturers, but they blame these on external forces, especially global businesses and trade liberalization. The key arguments here include accusations that other countries unfairly subsidize manufacturing, allow sweatshops that abuse and underpay their labour or employ other untoward tactics to lure manufacturing away from North America. The blamers are often anti-trade activists who believe far more damage than benefit has been inflicted on the world by trade liberalization. While there are certainly concerns around fair trade practices and labour standards, the overwhelming consensus of economists is that trade liberalization has done far more to raise living standards for millions around the world than has any other type of policy, including foreign aid.

The Blamers are the frog who externalizes the problem, doing nothing but croaking loudly and angrily, hoping someone on the outside of the pot will take pity and turn down the heat.

The IF ONLY-ers: A third camp agrees that Canadian manufacturers are in trouble, but insist these troubles could be solved through more favourable government policy measures. Of the three types of people likely to challenge the idea that manufacturing must change, the IF ONLY-ers are probably the most common. They see the solution lying in lobbying governments for tax concessions, more generous subsidies, loan guarantees and other domestic policy changes. Oddly, both union activists and management fall into this camp. Unions blame management for the problems and push for higher wages and better pensions (laudable goals, but not something that is going to improve the competitiveness of Canadian companies). Management blames unions for raising labour costs and imposing rigid, inflexible contracts. Both push government to do something, as witnessed in the 2008 auto bailout.

The solutions for those in this category all start the same way: "IF ONLY ....would do............, then the problems facing manufacturing would be solved." The IF ONLY-ers are the frog in the pot anxiously swimming around saying "if only the water was cooler."

Of course, all three are wrong. And like the frog that doesn't jump out of the pot, the IF ONLY-ers will find that their self-preservation strategies are going to end badly.

All is Not Lost!

So, is there a problem for Canadian manufacturing? Without question, the answer is yes. But there are reasons for hope, too.

First of all, to be clear, we are not suggesting that Canadian manufacturing is dead. We are, however, suggesting that unless some intentional changes happen, manufacturing could face a long, slow demise—not unlike the boiling frog. These changes are neither easy nor obvious. And although the IF ONLY-ers will be disappointed, these changes will require bigger thinking than just another government subsidy, tax break or loan guarantee.

Second, Canadians have to let go of the notion that Canada's manufacturing clout can return to what it was at its zenith in the 1960s and 1970s. They will have to accept the fact that if manufacturing is to continue playing a major role in the economy, it will look different. On the US side of the fence, the stories of Detroit and its long-time rival Chicago exemplify the difference in attitude. It is a bit of an oversimplification, but through the years Detroit held tightly to its role as auto king, hoping and praying that it would return, bashing the Japanese the whole time. Chicago, on the other hand, opened itself to a newer world, one that included not only new kinds of manufacturing, but also new industries and the arts.

Third, if Canada is to remain relevant in the sphere of manufacturing, Canadians will have to rethink where they want to be in the international value chain. As will be discussed in Chapter 8, the actual assemblage of merchandise—which is an outdated and incomplete concept of "manufacturing"—may not make sense for Canada. However, there are many other elements to manufacturing than just the assembly line and some of them have "Canada" written all over them.

Finally, there are enormous opportunities in high-quality, low-volume niche manufacturing. Germany, a country with high labour costs, demonstrates that it can be done. The Germans may not produce as many kitchen knives as the Chinese, for example, but the ones they do produce are of excellent quality and sell at a premium. Niche manufacturing may have a vibrant future in Canada. But to find those niches will take brains and lots of them. Designing, innovating, creating, marketing—all of these will have to play a much larger role in Canadian manufacturing in the future. These are not qualities that have typically characterized Canadian manufacturing. With some notable exceptions, the design and marketing of the goods was mostly done by foreign head offices of multi-national corporations. This arrangement served Canada well for a long time. But the world has changed and now Canadians must decide if they are going to continue to import other people's ideas for stuff to make or come up with ideas of their own. The latter is where the opportunities will be found.

While knowing full well change is required, Jayson Myers is more than optimistic about the future of manufacturing in Canada. But it's going to take some hard work:

> Canada's manufacturers cannot compete on the basis of low costs or economies of scale based on high volume production. The only way that our manufacturers can compete is by offering customers a specialized solution that differentiates them from competitors. Given the intense competition in production and technology development, that means value will be created primarily around design, logistics, time, reliability and customer services. All this calls for innovative products/services, new production and business processes, and the need to look for and follow customers to take advantage of market opportunities around the world.[8]

At face value, the statistics for manufacturing in Canada don't look great. But digging beneath the surface a bit reveals some interesting trends in manufacturing which yield a more hopeful outlook. A report from Statistics Canada shows that sales growth across twenty industry subgroups is anything but uniform.[9] Between 2000 and 2008, sales of manufactured goods in half of these industry subgroups were "expanding" while sales in the other half were "contracting." The expanding group includes sectors such as petroleum, chemicals and food. The contracting group includes textiles, computers and electronics, and automobiles.

These categories reveal two important things about manufacturing in Canada. One is that there are plenty of opportunities in some of the new, non-traditional manufacturing sectors, particularly those that feed into some of the specialized machinery and equipment required in natural resource extraction. The second important thing to observe from these categories is that there is a regional dimension to the expanding vs. contracting sectors. Central Canada has long been the dominant region of manufacturing in the country, but its major sectors—including autos—are among those facing the biggest contractions. The danger is that the east-west economic tensions could be exacerbated in the coming years.

Out With the Old

A few years ago, an AM radio call-in show in a small Canadian city was discussing the economy, how things are changing and what opportunities lay ahead. One mournful caller captured a sentiment that sadly typifies a lot of Canadians (and Americans, too): "We don't make anything anymore," he lamented. "What we need are people making things with their hands, or out in a field working with a hoe. We used to make stuff that people needed and bought. We don't make stuff anymore; we need to get that back."

His first observation was entirely correct: mostly, Canadians don't make as much stuff as they used to—not physical stuff, anyway, at least apart from harvesting resources. The idea of a "service-oriented" economy was, in his mind, clearly second rate, and he had a reason to worry. Wages in manufacturing and the "goods producing" sectors in the economy have traditionally been better paying. The fact that service sector jobs have been rising at a rate that more than offsets those lost in the goods producing sectors is little comfort when many of the service sector jobs are low-skill, low-paying "McJobs," a derogatory term popularized by Douglas Coupland's 1991 novel *Generation X*. It's understandable why many are worried and upset at the waning of traditional manufacturing.

But the caller was wrong in his recommendation that somehow Canadians have to get back to making stuff like they used to, and until they do, Canada will be underachieving economically. This nostalgia has got to go. Rather than replacing traditional, high-paying assembly line manufacturing jobs (i.e., manufacturing) with low-paying, low-skill jobs flipping hamburgers (i.e., services), this book suggests a positive vision of what the service sector can become.

Britain's Lost Blue Collar Eden

It's a reasonable, yet misguided, nostalgia that naturally leads one to yearn for the past, particularly the vibrant economic past of the post-war 1950s and 1960s. Canadians are not the only ones bemoaning the fact that traditional manufacturing—the big industrial plants, the assembly lines, the good-paying jobs—is not the primary driver of the economy anymore.

Take the UK, for example. Back in October 2009, Kenneth Clarke (a Conservative serving as the Opposition's shadow Business Secretary) complained that the problem facing the country was its lack of manufacturing. "Britain has to make things again," he said, pointing out that "in 12 years of Labour government, the number of manufacturing jobs in Britain has dropped by more than a third."[10] The comment came at a time of serious backlash against the British financial industry, which was left in tatters in the post-2008 credit meltdown.

Unfortunately, the term "services" had somehow become synonymous with the shady banking industry, which up until 2008 had been a major driver of the British economy. Now, the reputation of the financial services sector lay in ruins. The lament about Britain's manufacturing decline was echoed more recently by a member of the current Conservative government, the Chancellor of the Exchequer, George Osborne. While visiting a JCB Transmission plant (a transportation equipment manufacturer) in Wales in February 2011, the Chancellor said: "I think what we are starting to see is a manufacturing revival in Wales—and that is great. Wales needs to make things again."[11]

The phrase "make things again" was used by both politicians and it probably resonated with people. But the notion that traditional manufacturing—the "making things" model—will save the day for economies in the developed world is challenged by a respected British think tank, the National Endowment for Sciences, Technology and the Arts (NESTA). A research paper released in June 2010[12] outlines four key industrial growth scenarios for the UK to the year 2020. The first was a "business as usual" approach. In this scenario, manufacturing dwindles further vis-à-vis services. It could result in some economic growth, but unemployment would remain stubbornly high.

A second scenario—one in which manufacturing is emphasized and returned to 15% of the domestic economy (up from 12% currently)—would indeed improve employment and spark growth. However, the authors of the report suggest that this would require manufacturing to grow at 6.2% in the coming years, which they describe as improbable. "Such explosive growth is highly unlikely and would require growth of a scale not seen in recent times in the UK."[13] They also suggest that even in such a manufacturing renaissance, business services would still continue to grow more quickly and that manufacturing would result in negative impacts on other sectors through crowding out. Presumably, wage inflation and availability of labour would become a problem.

The report offers two other scenarios, however, with much more favourable outcomes for the UK economy: one is an emphasis on high-tech, and the other is a broadly-based innovation economy. These "knowledge economy" scenarios would result in robust economic growth (over 3.0% annually), and bring a faster rate of employment growth than either of the first two scenarios. The growth would also be spread more evenly across the regions of the UK. However, the authors add a caution that, while the high-tech and innovation scenarios are clearly more desirable, they would be "a stretch" to achieve. "They would require a number of factors to slot into place—the right skills in the economy, the ability to capitalize on external demand and significant private sector investment."[14] Obviously, they are easier said than done.

Time to Move On

The picture is clear. Canada's economy has been moving away from traditional manufacturing as its primary driver and relying more on the service sector and natural resources (more will be said about resources in the next chapter). There have been volumes of academic and analytical studies written about this, but in many ways it is self-evident: the world of mass manufacturing has moved on. The pot of water is heating up. And trying to get back to the good ol' days of manufacturing is a losing strategy. Canadians have to rethink and redefine the future for Canadian manufacturing. As Jayson Myers says, "business as usual is no longer an option."

In Part B, we discuss practical steps that businesses and individuals can take to ensure a bright economic future for Canada. Some of these steps require traditional manufacturers to see things in a new way. Other steps embrace the service sector, but in a way that creates good jobs. And others will result in creating new sectors of the economy that haven't even been discovered yet. In all cases, the steps will make use of an unlimited economic resource: brain power and the capacity to come up with new ideas.

Chapter 2

Natural Resources in the 21st Century

> "Now therefore ye are cursed, and there shall none of you be freed from being bondmen, and hewers of wood and drawers of water for the house of my God."
> — Joshua 9:23 (King James Version)

The Blessings

If Canada's manufacturing history goes back a ways, its history with natural resources goes back even further. European explorers and settlers didn't come to Canada for the great weather—they were chasing the riches they saw in fur trading. Decades later, settlements cropped up along the east coast and the St. Lawrence River, dominated by farming and forestry.

In the 20th century, it became obvious how ridiculously blessed Canada was in natural resources. Nickel, copper, iron ore, precious metals, asbestos, timber, hydro electricity—Canada seemed to have it all. And the rapidly industrializing and rebuilding economies of Europe and the United States needed what Canada had. Resource boom towns popped up across Quebec, Ontario, British Columbia and Manitoba in a mad rush to exploit these resources, and Canada prospered.

Pushing further west across the Prairies were waves of European settlers who farmed the land. By the 1950s, Canada had earned the nickname "Bread Basket to the World" because of its exports of high quality wheat and other cereals. Livestock and oilseeds such as canola followed. And Canada prospered.

Adding to this embarrassment of riches, in 1947, the Leduc #1 well struck an oil gusher, vaulting Alberta and Canada into the heady economic world of hydrocarbon extraction. Some sixty years later, Canada's Prime Minister was calling the country an "energy superpower." The global economy, thirsty for oil and gas, came calling. And Canada prospered some more.

Canada's economic history has been one dominated by its astounding abundance of natural resources. The blessings, of course, are cash and jobs. The global economy needs natural resources and it will pay to get them. This has without question improved Canada's terms of trade with the rest of the world.

The Curses

One curse is the boom-and-bust rollercoaster Canada's resource industries must ride as global prices for commodities go up and down over time. Many Canadian towns have suffered on this rollercoaster (Flin Flon, Sudbury and Prince George to name just a few). With massive stores of oil and gas, Alberta has an unlimited ticket to ride on the resource rollercoaster.

The second curse comes in the form of what economists call Dutch Disease. As the global price of a commodity rises, so too does the currency of a country that produces and exports this commodity. The rising currency can cause severe damage to other domestic industries (such as manufacturing) that can no longer compete globally with such a high currency.

A final curse is the common problem of countries selling their raw natural resources without benefitting from their secondary processing or upgrading. The lack of "value-added" industries is something that troubles many Canadians when they see their timber, iron ore, fish, oil and wheat shipped to other countries where they are turned into furniture, steel, fish sticks, gasoline, and pasta. Canadians disparagingly call themselves the world's "hewers of wood and drawers of water."

Reasons for Canadian Resource Producers to Worry

There are four global imperatives that are driving Canada's need to rethink the way it extracts resources, what it does with them, and how reliable they are as an economic engine.

1) The Politics of Carbon

It's not the purpose of this book to debate the science of climate change nor is it to pick a side on the usefulness of cutting Canada's carbon emissions. Rather, we start with a fact that is hard to dispute: governments around the world have identified carbon emissions as a major problem. Running parallel to this is the search for commercially viable alternatives to fossil fuel. This search is inspired by climate change but goes beyond it to include the desire for energy security and "cleaner" energy. In light of this, most agree that oil, gas and coal have a role to play in the global energy mix for years to come, but the jury is out on how big that role will be and how long it will last.

The war on carbon has turned into a cold war rather than the no holds barred version many environmentalists would like to see. The war on carbon, however, is far from over. Nor is Canada—a high per capita emitter of carbon and a major exporter of oil and gas to the United States—off the hook. The danger is that the ongoing push to reduce carbon consumption around the world will eventually hamstring the Canadian oil and gas industry.

2) International Competition

Despite the fact that Canada is almost ridiculously well-endowed with natural resources, it remains a small global player in almost every resource.[15] It is, in the words of an economist, a "price taker" in resources. Canada competes with the rest of the world in the extraction and transportation of resources and it faces some geographic disadvantages in this regard. Cost is everything and Canada's competitors are breathing down its neck.

3) Too Much of a Good Thing: Canada's Lack of Trade Diversity

It's no secret that Canada's economy is tied tightly to that of its largest and closest trading partner, the United States. The facts speak for themselves. In the ten years between 2001 and 2010, nearly 82% of all international merchandise exports from Canada were sold to the US. If there ever was a definition of trade dependency, this would be it. The heavy dependence on the US market is not quite as pronounced for Canada's natural resources, with 76.6% of resource exports going south of the border. Still, there is an unhealthy dependency on one market.

4) The Star Trek Solution: Potential Technological Breakthroughs in Energy

It wasn't that long ago when whale oil lamps were the norm along the US eastern seaboard and rock oil was a quirky substitute that most thought would never take off. The same was true for other innovations such as the horse and buggy (replaced by cars), the vacuum tube (replaced by microchips), and the fax machine (replaced by scanned email attachments).

Today, it seems unthinkable that the global economy could possibly move away from burning vast amounts of oil. But we may be one or two lucky accidents away from a revolution in how humans produce and consume energy. What if a game changing scientific discovery changes everything? What if the equivalent of the fictional *dilithium crystals* that powered the space ships in *Star Trek* come on line and render crude oil about as important as whale oil?

These four factors point to the need for Canada's natural resource producers to become even more creative and more innovative and how they can benefit from the ideas explored in Part B. Even though Canadians are not running out of resources any time soon, they can no longer just keep doing what they've always done, only more of it. Productivity needs to be increased in the face of foreign competition and Canadians need to extract their natural resources in ways that are environmentally acceptable to an increasingly critical global community. It's not enough for Canadians to glibly say "our oil is more ethical." Canada needs to be the best in the world at harvesting natural resources in environmentally sustainable ways. At the same time, Canada has to lessen its dependency on resource exports to the US. Because of geography, language and other factors, the US will remain Canada's largest trading partner for a long time. Canadians will, however, be missing out on lucrative opportunities in other global markets and they will remain tied to the fate of the US economy if they don't act quickly and decisively to tap other markets.

Good, But Not Good Enough

In addition to the global forces that are, or might be, aligned against Canada's natural resource industries, it needs to be recognized that natural resources alone cannot sustain an economy that must provide for 34 million Canadians. Yes, Canada's oil sands resource is an economic engine that directly and indirectly drives all sorts of economic activity throughout Canada. But even this huge resource is not enough to provide jobs in the future for *millions* of people.

And, notwithstanding the economic boost the oil sands provides for people in all parts of Canada, it really doesn't do that much for unemployed auto workers in Oshawa or potato farmers in PEI. And if the oil sands is not a sufficient engine, neither is a new nickel mine or some added agricultural capacity. These and other resource sector opportunities should be pursued, but they are not a sufficient substitute for the development of new economic engines.

External forces are heating the water in the pot. It's not Canada's fault. As Billy Joel sings: "we didn't start the fire." Nonetheless, Canadians have to find ways to get out of the water before it boils.

Chapter 3

The Tightly-Knit Global Economy

> "World economies are now linked inextricably, spreading wealth further and faster than ever before. There is no turning back on global connectedness; we must learn to deal with crises collectivity by strengthening global and regional relationships."
> — PricewaterhouseCoopers[16]

The Butterfly Effect

In chaos theory, scientists describe what is popularly called the butterfly effect—the idea that because of the interdependence of complex systems, a small, seemingly irrelevant event in one system can result in enormous, unpredictable consequences in related systems. The term has been used in meteorology—a butterfly's wings might create tiny changes in the atmosphere that could, through a series of changes along the way, alter the path of a tornado. It's also been used by chaos theorists in physics, astronomy and, of course, economics and finance.

Today, the economy seems more susceptible to the wild and sometimes gut-wrenching interdependencies of global commerce. Irwin Stelzer, Director of Economic Policy Studies at the Hudson Institute in Washington D.C., sums it up in an online interview with BBC World Service:

> Anyone who doubts that we live in an interconnected world—some call it globalization—hasn't been following the economic news. Greece catches a cold, and all of the 16 nations that make up Euroland sneeze. The American Federal Reserve Board's monetary policy gurus decide to print more money—some call it quantitative easing, or QE—and the entire group of G20 nations rises in indignation as the dollar falls. China expands so rapidly that its demand for fuel and food skyrocket, and consumers around the world watch prices at petrol stations and in supermarkets rise. The North Korean regime shows off its nuclear stock and lobs some lethal shells into South Korean territory, and there is a worldwide flight to the safe haven of the dollar—the same currency that investors shunned just a short time ago. And German chancellor Angela Merkel says that from now on investors in countries and banks that go broke will have to bear some of the losses—some call that a haircut—and the price of Eurozone bonds jumps. It seems that we are all in the same boat, and that it is taking on water at an uncomfortable rate. Repair one leak, and the ship springs another.[17]

A housing market collapse in Arizona leads to Iceland going bankrupt. An iPod designed in America is assembled in China and sold around the world. A bank in France sets in motion events that crack the retirement nest egg of seniors in British Columbia. An offhand comment by the Assistant Deputy Finance Minister of Hungary causes the Canadian dollar to tumble. A decision to sell Venezuelan heavy oil to China causes American companies to scrap plans for an oil upgrader in Alberta.

All are examples of the bizarre and seemingly uncontrollable world in which we all now live. Globalization—a term that has been around for many decades already—has gone beyond a simple reference to international trade in merchandise. It now refers to the complex, often seamless web through which billions of dollars move in an instant. We are truly connected, at least economically.

This raises both concerns and opportunities.

The concerns are obvious. Does an increasingly globalized world imply that we are less and less in control of our own national sovereignty and destiny? Do our political leaders need to worry more about how foreign governments and corporations may react to certain policies? Are the desires and interests of Canadians becoming secondary? These are valid questions, and if not addressed properly, they will incite fear. In the extreme, they lead some Canadians to want to close the borders to global trade.

The problem is that Canada finds itself part of this tightly-knit "butterfly effect" economy if it likes it or not. Assuming Canadians don't give in to the fear mongers by closing the borders to trade and commerce, they have two choices: hunker down and fearfully hope for the best when it comes to doing business abroad or become much more cosmopolitan and understand what makes the world beyond Canada's borders tick.

Like the frog in the pot of *cool* water, cocooning is a safe strategy. Nothing from outside the pot can get it, and the water within the pot can't get out. All is well. But when the water within the pot starts to warm up, cocooning is no longer a safe option. In fact, it will prove to be fatal if no action is taken.

Global Trade

Trade of goods and services around the globe accounts for a massive portion of the world's economy. Exports from the advanced economies alone in 2008 totaled just over $US 10.7 trillion, and imports over $US 9.8 trillion (see Figure 1).[18] Those figures did fall by about 20% during the 2009 global recession, however, reflecting not only the drop of economic activity but also the knee-jerk reaction of the many countries that responded to a faltering economy by imposing import barriers. Global trade did make some gains in 2010, recovering just over half the losses in trade from the previous year. However, global trade still remains below pre-recession levels.

Emerging economies are also heavily involved in global trade, although it is still dwarfed by imports and exports from the advanced economies. Trade from developing Asian economies has more than recovered from the recession, with exports amounting to $US 2.4 trillion in 2010 (up from $US 2.0 trillion in 2008), and just under $US 3.0 trillion in imports (up from $2.8 trillion in 2008).

Surprisingly, developing Asian economies as a whole still import more than they export, although many individual countries (notably China) may have trade surpluses. This reflects the dependence on raw materials such as crude oil, forestry products and base metals being imported by the emerging Asian nations for their own industrial and manufacturing needs.

FIGURE 1: Total Global Trade – Exports and Imports by Region to All Trade Partners ($US billions)

EXPORTS	2008	2009	2010
Advanced Economies	10682.1	8108.14	9522.89
Emerging and Developing Countries	5130.59	4043.82	5207.83
Developing Asia	2022.31	1762.6	2405.09
Europe	1277.39	811.39	1016.91
Middle East and North Africa	710.46	588.66	656.55
Sub-Saharan Africa	271.98	221.89	261.59
Western Hemisphere	852.04	661.42	870.5
IMPORTS			
Advanced Economies	9813.41	7659.17	8980.09
Emerging and Developing Countries	6526.17	4927.65	6308.49
Developing Asia	2774.78	2332.06	2979.93
Europe	1237.5	870.41	1084.76
Middle East and North Africa	1237.5	730.31	956.69
Sub-Saharan Africa	362.19	244.03	319.17
Western Hemisphere	989.22	758.98	978.32

Source: IMF eLibrary data (http://elibrary-data.imf.org/DataReport.aspx?c=1449299&d=33061&e=170921)

Despite overwhelming empirical evidence and a nearly unanimous opinion among economists that global trade has helped improve the living standards for millions of citizens round the world, there are many voices opposed to global trade. In fact, the term "globalization" itself is often used in the pejorative, a kind of dirty word blamed for many of the problems faced by the emerging economies. Poor working conditions, environmental degradation, cycles of poverty and almost every other ill facing the third world are blamed on global trade with the developed nations.

Without question, there are issues to be solved. The profit motivation of global corporations, if left unchecked, can cause problems and be the source of abuse. But those are issues that can be solved through appropriate regulation and laws. Attacking global trade itself as the source of the problem is throwing the baby out with the bath water. Canada needs to trade, a fact that will become even more evident in the coming decades.

In 2010, the province of Alberta set out looking for some ideas on how to secure its economic edge. At the request of Premier Ed Stelmach, a group of high profile individuals was asked to come up with recommendations that could shape Alberta's economy—grand visions and ideas that would ensure the province's prosperity and quality of life in the future. In May 2011, the Premier's Council for Economic Strategy released a report entitled *Shaping Alberta's Future*.

The Council identified five key areas and made a series of recommendations. In the preamble to its report, the group of experts emphasizes the opportunities to expand trade relations into Asia and South America:

> … we also see potential opportunities in the growing economies of Central and South America. GDP growth in Latin American countries has outstripped the OECD average in fourteen of the past twenty years. Average growth across Latin America is double that of Canada. There are countries in resource-based South America that share our interest in energy and mining, agriculture and biosciences, as well as the related challenges.

> By 2040, for example, Brazil is projected to become the world's fourth largest economy. It is home to one of the world's largest oil companies, Petrobras. While Brazil has been considered a competitor to Canada's agriculture products, it is a potential partner in the search for cleaner energy. What Brazil needs most is assistance with education and training, something Alberta's education system and our larger companies could provide.

> We have noted the shift in the economic centre of gravity to Asia, and the major influence of China and India in the global economy. Both

countries are investing strategically around the world—particularly in Africa—to secure long-term supplies of energy, food and other primary resources to meet the needs of 1.3 billion people in China, 1.2 billion in India and expanding middles classes. Other Asian countries such as Vietnam, Sri Lanka and Indonesia are also on a rapid growth track.[19]

The advice of the Council is clear: diversity in trade—and expansion of trade in services such as education—will help ensure a bright economic future. And while the Council was writing the report in reference to Alberta, the message is perfectly applicable to any other of the nine provinces or three territories in the country.

Canada's Role in the Global Economy

Canadians already like to think of their country as an export-oriented one. But as the discussion on manufacturing and natural resources in Chapters 1 and 2 describe, Canada has been more of a supplier to the US economy than a true global player. This will have to change in the future if Canada is going to continue to prosper. But how?

Global trade is not only increasing, it's becoming more complex and nuanced. It is no longer good enough for a producer anywhere to say "Here's what I make," find a buyer, and call himself a global trader. That may have worked for much of the 20th century—but in the 21st century, global traders will have to find ways to become a part of the global chain of production.

Consider the automotive industry. It used to be possible to categorize car companies by country: Ford is a US car maker; Toyota is a Japanese car maker; Renault is a French car maker, etc. But increasingly, this makes no sense. Certainly the head office of the car company remains fixed to one particular country. But in the 21st century, a car could be designed in Japan, with computer engineering systems from Switzerland, parts made in Brazil, Mexico and South Korea, an engine built by a German company, marketing campaigns plotted in Japan, the UK and California, environmental and safety testing by a Swedish company, and final assembly in Alabama. The car could then be sold by a retailer in Chicago and run on gasoline made from Alberta's oil sands.

Hardly a "Japanese" car anymore, is it? Increasingly, products are becoming seamlessly global in their design and assembly. And like firms in every other country, Canadian businesses are going to have to figure out where they can best fit into that seamless chain of production. It may not even be the export of a particular part, or even the provision of some high-knowledge service like engineering (although these are common). It could even be the export of a better, more logical and more efficient method of doing something. Logistics and management expertise have huge potential as exports from Canada to the world.

Sarah Kutulakos, Executive Director and Chief Operating Officer of the Canada China Business Council, understands this nuance. "The companies that thrive, she says, 'get their heads around the fact that participating in today's global value chain is not just sourcing and selling. It's thinking about what a market needs and how you can supply it. ... A lot of companies may have a product that isn't interesting to a country like China but the expertise in bringing it to market efficiently is something they might need.'"[20]

Much more will be said about moving up the global economic supply chain in Chapter 8, including how Canadian companies will have to change their habits and thinking.

Butterfly Net

The global economy is becoming more interconnected all the time, and as it does, the butterfly effect is felt: one action or event in one part of the world can have an enormous impact on another, seemingly unrelated part. Global trade, while it did stumble a bit in the 2008-09 recession, is without question an integral part of the world's economy. The term "globalization" has tended to galvanize economists and activists alike—the former using the term to describe how millions have been lifted out of poverty while the latter use it as a term of derision and a whipping boy for all the shortcomings and miseries in the world.

While recognizing the dizzying speed at which globalization is transforming the world—and the pain and injustices that capitalism can sometimes impose—we firmly believe that a prosperous, sustainable and environmentally responsible society will find its future in stronger global ties. Canada is no exception to these trends; indeed, because of its small population size (Canada is not tiny like Lithuania or Qatar, but it is much smaller than the big boys it wants to play with like China, the US and Germany) and modest international stature, Canada will need to embrace globalization more enthusiastically than other nations.

But embracing international business and commerce doesn't come naturally for many Canadians—at least not when we think of "international" as being beyond the United States. Canadians have some catching up to do in marketing Canada as a global brand name.

To update a well-known saying, the highly-connected and economically vibrant world is Canada's oyster! Canada has all that it needs to be smart, nimble, and competitive. If the global economy is heating up the water inside the pot, Canada needs to change its economic DNA so it can not only jump out of the pot but thrive in the world outside it. Part B of this book discusses how this can be done.

Chapter 4

Flying Under the Radar

"The average Indian would not know much about Canada except that this is a country which is a neighbour of the US."
— Sunaina Singh, President of the Shastri Indo-Canadian Institute

Canada the Invisible?

One of the world's most read and respected magazines, *The Economist*, does an annual issue focusing on the year to come. The cover of *The World in 2011*, an issue printed in December 2010, is cleverly designed as a mosaic of pictures from newsmakers around the world. Images of people from the US, the UK, and China are prominent. There are photos of Nicholas Sarkozy, Hillary Clinton, Angela Merkel and Vladimir Putin. The President of Chile smiles on the cover.

There are images of wind turbines, a graphic of global population growth and an Olympic athlete. Australian Prime Minister Julia Gillard is featured, as is the New Zealand rugby team. Even celebrity chef Jamie Oliver gets his picture on the cover. The largest and most prominent photo is reserved for the biggest news maker of all: US President Barrack Obama.

The World in 2011 has 166 pages of stories about different countries. Canada manages to receive one single page of attention—about the same amount of ink reserved for countries like Cuba, Ghana, and Croatia.

Canada is, according to *The Economist's* year-end issue anyway, virtually invisible.

Granted, *The Economist* is just a magazine and the 2011 year-end edition is just one issue. What its lack of coverage about Canada says is perhaps not all that significant. It is admittedly anecdotal evidence of Canada's relative standing in the international community. But it is evidence nonetheless. In this widely read and highly respected publication, the world is being given the message that Canada is about as interesting or as important as Croatia (no offence to Croatia). This is not good enough if Canada is to be the world's go to business partner, education provider and immigrant destination.

Scan the BBC World News website and you'll be hard pressed to find any news about Canada (notwithstanding negative news such as the Vancouver hockey riot in June 2011). Smaller countries such as Norway, Australia, Switzerland and South Africa are regularly featured.

Despite being one of the top ten largest global stock exchanges in terms of capitalization, Canada's TSX is never reported on the business tickers of CNN, the BBC or MSNBC—while much smaller exchanges in New Zealand and Sweden are.

Global consumers identify IKEA with Sweden, Corona with Mexico, Nokia with Finland, and LEGO with Denmark. As author Andrea Mandel-Campbell asks in her book *Why Mexicans Don't Drink Molson*, how is it that Mexico—a country not known for barley or fresh water—has been able to parlay its brand of beer into the 4th largest in the world? Canadian beer brands, on the other hand, barely dent the global beer market.

Why is it that for a country of over 34 million people and an economy still comfortably within the top ten or fifteen in the world, Canada commands relatively little international attention? There are exceptions: for example, Canada recently garnered top spot in a ranking by *Forbes* of the best countries for business.[21] The fact that this was a surprise to many people suggests that the exceptions prove the rule. This needs to change. Canada has to start punching above its weight when it comes to international attention.

This chapter will explore the extent to which the rest of the world thinks about Canada and Canadians. The emphasis will not be on *what* they think—there's plenty of evidence to suggest most of the world thinks that Canadians are a generally swell bunch—but rather *how much* they think about Canada at all.

Are We Really Being Ignored?

Before Canadians can get too excited about the world ignoring them, let's take a step backward to determine whether this is fact or fiction. Of course, unlike population statistics or ordinary economic data like GDP, there is no common numeric measurement of how much other countries pay attention to each other. Because of the very subjective nature of the question "How often does the rest of the world think about Canada?" there is going to be no definitive, quantifiable answer.

However, there are plenty of sources that rank countries by various attributes or produce "Top 10" or "Top 100" lists. What follows is a quick snapshot of Canada's profile or ranking in seven key areas:

→ international media coverage;
→ quality of life;
→ cities;
→ the arts;

→ geography;
→ designers; and
→ universities.

The sources were chosen because they are foreign-based. The idea here is to get a rough sense of Canada's international profile. It is by no means scientific; still, it reveals some interesting trends that are hard to ignore.

International Media Coverage

Let's return to a closer and more thorough examination of coverage in *The Economist* magazine. Based in London but with wide global distribution, it is arguably the world's most recognized and widely read magazine on politics, business and economics. Run a search on *The Economist* online edition for country names mentioned in the title of the article, and Canada comes up in the title of 4,678 articles since January 2000.

That puts us well below the United States (83,130 articles) and the UK (27,703), which shouldn't be surprising given the political and economic clout held by these two countries. (The UK's high ranking probably has more to do with geographic bias since *The Economist* is based in London.) Other countries that rank highly are China, France and Germany—large countries that generate a lot of economic and political news relevant to the rest of the world. Canada, however, ranks among some not-so-heavyweight countries like South Africa, Mexico, Australia and Ireland.

If you add to the article count for each county the number of mentions of the largest city and capital—which captures mentions in titles for New York/Washington, Toronto/Ottawa, London, Paris, Tokyo, Berlin and Rome—Canada's ranking is decidedly last among its G7 peers. New York alone registers 16,486 mentions in article titles, while Toronto ekes out a mere 856.

On the surface, it's tempting to file a complaint that the rest of the world does indeed ignore Canada—or at least that *The Economist* finds Canada quite uninteresting and non-newsworthy. But is this out of line with the reality of Canada's size? Its population of 34 million is just over half the size of the next largest G7 country—Italy, with about 60 million. Yet Canada's combined mentions is actually quite close to matching those of Italy (despite that country having a much more colourful and notorious leader). According to the International Monetary Fund, Canada's GDP ranked 9th in the global economy in 2010, and if you exclude Israel and Iran from the list, that's close to the ranking that Canada receives in terms of total articles in *The Economist*.

As for Canada's ranking relative to the US/New York/Washington, arguably America's weight and influence in the global economics and politics is indeed twenty times greater than is Canada/Toronto/Ottawa.

So judging by stories appearing in *The Economist*, it is difficult to make a strong case that Canada is really being ignored too badly. Canada is after all, a small and calm country and it appears to be appearing in its fair share of article titles relative to the size of its population and GDP.

Quality of Life

By most measures, Canada is doing very well relative to the rest of the world. And that, at least, seems to be recognized by its global peers. Canada is consistently ranked among the very highest in the United Nations' Human Development Index, placing 8th in 2010.[22] That is down from the #1 or #2 spot Canada routinely held throughout the 1990s. The best country in the world in 2010 was Norway, followed by Australia, New Zealand, the United States, Ireland, Lichtenstein and the Netherlands. Sweden and Germany follow Canada, to round out the top 10.

While Canada's fall down to a lowly eighth place may be unsettling, the countries at the top of the index are separated by very small differences. Basically, anything in the top 10 is essentially equal in terms of human development and standard of living.

As well, according to the World Economic Forum, Canada is a reasonably competitive place economically. Judging by a series of criteria—institutions, infrastructure, macroeconomic environment, health and primary education, higher education and training, goods market efficiency, labour market efficiency, financial market development, technological readiness, market size, business sophistication and innovation—Canada ranked 15th in the world.[23] That was a drop from 9th place overall in 2009, and even higher rankings in previous years. Nonetheless, it puts Canada in some fairly good company, and the difference between the rankings (as with the UN Human Development Index) is quite small.

We've got great cities, as well. In rankings of the best cities in the world, Canadian cities often rank near the top. Two examples are the Mercer Quality of Living Survey and *The Economist*'s World's Most Liveable Cities rankings. In the 2010 Mercer rankings, Vancouver places fourth in the world.[24] In *The Economist's* 2011 rankings, three Canadian cities—Vancouver (1st), Toronto (4th) and Calgary (5th)—place in the top five cities in the world for liveability.[25]

Less favourable yet still respectable, *Monocle* magazine ranked Vancouver 16th and Montreal 19th of the top 25 cities in the world in 2011.[26]

Cities

But Canada and Canadian cities are not always ranked so favourably. Even worse, sometimes they're *not ranked at all*.

The influential Knight Frank, a leading global provider of services and consulting on residential and commercial property, hardly recognizes Canadian cities exist. In the 2011 Knight Frank Global Cities Survey, only one Canadian city, Toronto, makes it on the list of "40 Best Cities in the World." (It ranked 10th). No other Canadian city was even mentioned, not even Vancouver or Montreal. Apparently they were beat out by global cities such as Istanbul (#27), Bogota (#35) and even Jakarta (#39).[27]

The Knight Frank survey attempts to rank cities according to their "provision of investment opportunities and their influence on global business leaders and the political elite." Cities are evaluated in four categories, all of which are quite extensive in capturing the strengths and weaknesses of each metro:

1) economic activity, including economic output, income per head, financial and capital market activity and market share and the number of international business headquarters in each city;

2) political power, which calculates the number of headquarters for national political organizations, international non-governmental organizations, embassies and think tanks;

3) quality of life, measuring personal and political freedom, censorship, personal security, crime, political stability, health facilities, public service, transportation, culture, leisure, climate, and the quality of the natural and man-made environment; and

4) knowledge and influence, which assesses educational status, the number of educational facilities, national and international media organizations, news bureaus and the international market share of locally-based media.

Toronto manages to eke out a respectable #10 spot overall because it ranks very high (#3) in terms of quality of life. However, it fails to make the list at all for economic activity, political power or knowledge and influence.

It is easy to see how Toronto can rank lower than cities like London, New York, Los Angeles and Singapore on political power, influence, or economic activity. But how is it that Toronto falls behind cities like Mexico City on political power? Or Sydney on knowledge and influence? And why is it that Canadian cities like Vancouver and Montreal are not even mentioned at all, yet cities with similar (or smaller) populations like Milan, Johannesburg, Frankfurt and Zurich are all in the Top 40?

There are three possible responses to this.

The first is that the Knight Frank survey is simply garbage. Clearly if Johannesburg ranks as a "better" city than Vancouver, the research is so hopelessly flawed that it isn't worth worrying about. This is a clear possibility.

The second possibility is that, due to practical space or resource constraints, the survey purposely included only one representative city from Canada. And as the largest and most visible, Toronto is an obvious choice. This is possible, although it doesn't explain why it includes seven US cities, three German cities, and two Brazilian cities. And it also doesn't explain why the survey claims to capture the Top Cities in the World—a name that implies it is blind to national boundaries. Otherwise, the survey would be called "The Top City in Each Country of the World."

The third is that the report is in fact accurate, but sadly Canadian cities just don't cut it. This is also possible, especially considering some of the criteria that the Knight Frank report emphasizes, such as international business headquarters and international media organizations. Canadians may want to quibble with the selection of these criteria, arguing that these sorts of things don't make cities "great." But it is Knight Frank's survey, not theirs.

The fourth possibility is that Canadian cities didn't make it into the rankings because (other than Toronto) they were never top-of-mind for the designers of the survey. Presumably, the team working on the report had to start with a list of global cities. It's very likely that cities such as Vancouver, Montreal or Calgary were never included in the rankings simply because no one thought to include them.

Of these four possibilities, the fourth seems most likely. Canada is so invisible that its major cities hardly merit a mention in global rankings. It should come as no surprise, therefore, that Johannesburg ranks above Montreal, or Jakarta above Vancouver, as "great" global cities. Canadian cities don't make the list in the first place because no one even thought to rank them.

The news from the Knight Frank "Best Cities in the World" report gets even worse. When subjectively asked about which cities will rank among the greatest in ten years time, Toronto—the one and only Canadian city to make the rankings in 2011—falls off the list entirely. The implication is that other cities such as Geneva, San Francisco, Zurich, Sao Paulo and Mumbai are expected to become the great cities of the future, and Canada will be completely shut out.

The Arts

Setting aside the fuss about Canada's lack of ranking with the global big boys in terms of political influence or economic clout, how about the arts? Here too, sadly, there is not much evidence that Canadians are getting noticed as much as they will need to be if they hope to known as top flight global players. And it is not a good idea to dismiss this as "their loss" because it's also Canada's loss.

Take for example a website called World Reviewer (www.worldreviewer.com). Based in London, the website markets itself as a resource for helping world travellers find "the best holiday ideas and travel experiences all over the world." The site offers a comprehensive list of notable museums, art galleries and cultural sites from around the world, listing 385 "experiences." Ranked at the top of the list are the expected: the Lourve in Paris, the Hermitage in St. Petersburg and the British Museum in London. The MOMA in New York and the National Gallery in Washington D.C. round out the top five museums in the world. Further down the list, museums in Egypt, the Netherlands, Austria and Italy are mentioned.

No Canada.

Are We Really That Different?

Canadian cities have often thought of themselves as world class, despite perhaps being somewhat small in size relative to some of their international competitors. But are we that unique? Notable citizens in one particular city were asked a few questions about the strengths and challenges that this particular urban area is facing. Consider the responses and see if you can guess the city in question.

Population: 965,000

TO BECOME A TRULY GLOBAL CITY, IT WILL NEED TO:
" Build upwards rather than outwards to protect green areas."
" Obsess less about being such a small city."

THE BEST THING ABOUT LIVING HERE IS:

" It is an outdoor city with mountains on the doorstep."

" In the summertime, I can walk 50m from my office in the central business district and be on the river"

" The city has changed substantially in the past two decades due to intelligent legislation and an influx of global culture."

THE BIGGEST OPPORTUNITY FOR THE CITY IS:

" To respect urbanism on a landscape sale. If its population were to rise significantly, it would lose many of its qualities."

" To continue benefiting from the drift away from inefficient, strike-prone and frustrating mega-cities like those found elsewhere on the continent."

" For people from all over the world to live here and make a real contribution to urban diversity."

" To further develop its strengths as a knowledge society."

Sounds a lot like the comments you'd hear about Calgary, Alberta. But if that was your guess, you'd be wrong. In fact, the city is Zurich, Switzerland. It was ranked #22 in the "Best Cities in the World" list. In ten years time, it is expected to climb to #13.

So the question is, why is Calgary not on the list?

Fair enough, one could argue. Canada is a much smaller country than the US, France or Russia, and it doesn't have the same sense of cultural history as countries like Austria and Holland.

If you keep scrolling down the list of Top 385 Museums in the world, you see countries like Australia, Belgium, Thailand, Mexico (2 in the top 20 rankings), Germany and Israel. Plenty more museums from the United States, the UK, and Russia keep popping up. A museum in Peru comes in at #48. Sweden, Cuba and Vietnam roll by, as do New Zealand and Norway.

Finally—at #70, just behind the Viking Ship Museum in Olso—we find the Canadian Museum of Civilization in Gatineau, Quebec. Ranking #99, just behind a museum in Vilnius, Lithuania is Canada's National Gallery in Ottawa.

And then... that's it! Apparently, Canada has only two museums worth visiting. Of the top 385 museums, we are outpaced by almost everyone, including much smaller countries like Morocco (8), Australia (8), Sweden (7), Finland (6), New Zealand (5), Costa Rica (3), Cambodia (3), Malta (3), Columbia (3) and Belgium (3). With two museums ranked in the top

385, we are tied with heavyweights like Ireland, Portugal, and the United Arab Emirates. (But we have twice as many museums worth visiting as Mongolia and Armenia, both of which have only one!)

As with the Knight Frank survey of great cities in the world, it is possible that the World Reviewer website is a shoddy online resource. How could its reviewers miss mentioning the Art Gallery of Ontario, the Musée d'art contemporain de Montréal, or the Museum of Anthropology on the campus of the University of British Columbia? These are world class art museums, aren't they? If World Reviewer missed these, then clearly it is not a reliable source.

While this premise could be true, it sounds a bit like how some economists respond when their models do not give the expected outcomes—"there must be something wrong with the data!" It's not scientific, but as a globally respected source for tourists looking for great travel experiences, The World Reviewer is as good a source as any.

Another possibility is that Canadian art and culture museums (other than the two mentioned in the Capital Region) are just not up to world class standards. After all, the World Reviewer website does have details on 385 museums around the world. They found museums in Estonia and Mongolia! Clearly they've done their homework.

Or it could be that because Canada is a relatively new country, we don't have the same amount of historic or cultural significance as do older countries (especially in Europe). But this doesn't hold water, either. For one thing, Canada's Aboriginal peoples and their culture have been around a lot longer than the art work hanging in The Louvre. Also, Canada—at 144 years old—is not that young anymore; politically younger countries like Australia and New Zealand have more museums and galleries on the list. Finally, many of the museums listed are contemporary art galleries like the MOMA. Canada's age is really irrelevant.

Finally, it's possible that World Reviewer is a perfectly legitimate online resource, but it didn't include the six or seven Canadian museums that deserve to be in the Top 385 ranking because they simply didn't think about Canada at all. If this is the case, it means that Canada has lots to offer but it needs to make sure that the rest of the world knows about it and appreciates it.

(In an email correspondence with the editors of World Reviewer, we inquired as to why only two Canadian museums made their list. In a very polite response, the editor indicated that her global list depends on two main sources of information: 1) submissions from people in various countries who want to recommend their own domestic museums; and 2) people who have traveled to museums in other countries and thought them worthy of the list. The editor mentioned that she has heard from hardly any Canadians about Canada's museums and that other international museum visitors don't talk about Canada. To help rectify the situation, we recommended seven additional Canadian museums that should be on their list. The editor kindly thanked us for our suggestions.)

In fact, Canada does have world-class museums, but they fly so far beneath the global radar screen that no one knows about them. Even worse, Canadians don't bother to promote their own museums to the rest of the world. Both are problems and symptomatic of Canada's invisibility. If Canada is seen as a vast Siberia-like land covered in ice and dotted with igloos (a sense of the country offered by a businessman from Mexico), it will not only punch below its weight on international lists, but also in the economic arena where awareness of where opportunities lie is critical. "Never heard of it" is not going to bring capital, talent or visitors to Canada.

Geography

OK, so Canada's cities lack political influence and they don't have well-known museums. That's why Canada has been under-represented in surveys of the great urban and cultural destinations of the world. Canada is a country of geography—soaring mountains, unimaginable open spaces, formidable tundra, stunning oceans. That's what the country is about, and that's what the world knows about it. Right?

Consider one of the most well-known photographic art exhibitions in the world, the "Earth from the Air" project, a spectacular presentation of large scale photographs of astonishing natural landscapes. Created by world-famous photographer Yann Arthus-Bertrand, every stunning aerial photograph portrays a unique, interesting location shot from high above. The exhibit travels around the world, showing in outdoor locations such as the grounds near the Natural History Museum in London, le Jardin du Luxembourg in Paris and the Millennium Park in Chicago.

These images are as good as natural photography gets, blending geography with art. Represented are locations from around the globe including France, Egypt, Paraguay, England, India, Kenya, Holland, Thailand, Denmark, Maldives, Greece, Jordan, Argentina, Indonesia and Mauritania. The United States is represented at least 20 times. There are dozens and dozens of photos, each a testament to the beauty and majesty of the earth.

Canada is represented by only one photo, entitled "The Ice-Breaker Louis Saint Laurent in Resolute Bay, Nunavut Territory." While it is a gorgeous photo, the obvious question is why in the entire collection of the earth's natural geography, Canada—the second largest country in the world with a land mass as varied and interesting as any—would merit only one picture?

It's not as if there are no natural features in Canada that are worthy of photography. Nor is it possible that Canada was too remote or difficult to locate on the map. Even if the 100 pictures were taken randomly around the globe, Canada's immense geography alone would, statistically, merit four or five photos.

Tempering the "Earth from the Air" project, Canadian geography does a bit better in another well-respected source of geography. But only a bit. Lonely Planet's *The Traveler's Guide to Planet Earth* features the fifty most extraordinary destinations in the world, inspired by the BBC series of documentaries *Planet Earth*. In the most recent edition, Canada is featured three times among the 50 most extraordinary destinations: the great salmon run in Knight Inlet, British Columbia; the endless herds of caribou in the Canadian Arctic; and the majesty of the Rocky Mountains (although we share billing with the US on this one).

Three mentions among the top 50 "most extraordinary" geographical destinations in the world isn't too bad, although the US still manages seven mentions. While it is a marginally smaller country in size, it is more varied geographically than is Canada, so perhaps this isn't too out of line. And again, the point is not to challenge The Lonely Planet and the BBC Planet Earth folks for leaving out other amazing geographic wonders of this country (Gros Morne National Park in Newfoundland and The Bay of Fundy in New Brunswick come to mind.) The point is to simply observe that they picked 50 extraordinary geographic spots in the world, but only three of them are in Canada.

Designers

One of the most important indicators of economic prosperity and innovation, of which much more will be said in Chapter 5, is the field of design. This can be anything from software design and industrial design to interior design to urban planning. The basic task of any designer is to solve a problem, find the best way to represent something and to do so in a way that pleases our aesthetic senses.

As a proxy for design in general, consider graphic design—the basic underpinnings of commercial advertising and visual communications. In 2009, European author and graphic designer Maia Francisco produced the *Atlas of Graphic Designers*. In this intriguing volume, Francisco identifies the top 100 or so graphic artists in the world, profiling their work, styles and influences. One of the most unique aspects of the book is a stylized map for each artist showing the cities to which the artist has a connection. Flipping through the several hundred page book reveals a very interesting pattern of the cities and countries which are at the forefront of contemporary graphic design.

Cities may be listed multiple times as places of influence on an artist. New York was the most frequently identified city in the geography of influence with almost 50 "hits" from artists who at some point spent time there. New York was followed by, not surprisingly, cities like London, Paris and Tokyo—all large and clearly dominant cities at the forefront of graphic design—each with between 20 and 30 mentions.

But smaller cities are also notable centres of graphic design. Olso had 11 hits; Stockholm, Copenhagen and Helsinki had 6 each. Even some less likely cities were mentioned such as Sao Paolo (5), Shanghai (5), Tel Aviv (5), Zagreb (5) and Mexico City (4). All told, 171 global cities are listed—most of them multiple times—as having had some sort of influence on the creative design of the top graphic artists of the world. Counting the multiple hits, there are well over 500 connections to various cities.

Of these 500+ city hits, Canada scores only 5—Montreal, Quebec City, Edmonton, Vancouver, and Bowen Island, BC. Montreal received two hits, which means that two of the world's best graphic designers have had some connection with the city. Edmonton's one hit doesn't really count—it was the birth place of one of the featured designers, but the artist has left (and apparently has never returned to Edmonton to work or live). And while Bowen Island, BC is a hotbed of artistry and design, it is a relatively tiny community. Really only three cities—Montreal, Quebec City and Vancouver—have had any sort of real connection or influence with the world's greatest commercial designers and even these ties are fairly loose.

Why is it that a city like Toronto, which prides itself as a centre of modern culture, should have registered zero connections with world-renowned graphic artists? Even Orlando, Florida—not a place that leaps to mind when thinking about cutting edge art or design—has two hits. Canada's largest city and cultural centre is completely missing from the atlas.

Size of city is clearly not a factor here, so it's not valid to suggest that Canada's cities are too small to be very influential centres of design. Toronto's census metropolitan population of 5 million is more than six times the size of Zagreb, Croatia (800,000), yet Zagreb beats Toronto 5-0. Vancouver's 2 million is also more than six times the size of The Hague, Holland (476,000), but Vancouver managed only 1 hit compared to 5 for The Hague. Based on population alone, then, The Hague outpaces Vancouver by a factor of twenty!

Ruling out population as a factor leaves three other possible explanations as to why Canada appears to be a design wasteland.

The first is that Canadians simply don't emphasize "design" as something worth pursuing, so therefore we've never really produced great designers nor have we thought it worthwhile to actively attract them. The second is that the top global designers do not consider Canadian cities as places in which to find inspiration, to study, or enjoy camaraderie with other artists. (Remember that the atlas of design lists not only the hometowns of the artists, but all cities with which they've made a connection over their careers.) Third is that Canada has great designers and its cities would be worthy of hosting great designers from around the world, but both are secrets too well kept. Either we are substandard or we are invisible. Given the importance of cultivating and attracting creative human capital and knowledge businesses, neither bodes well for Canada's economic future.

Universities

Yet another international ranking is that of universities. Quacquarelli Symonds Limited (QS) is a company specializing in education and study abroad. It is well-respected for research on, and ranking of, top global universities. Populating the top five positions are schools from the UK and the US: University of Cambridge, Harvard University, Yale University, University College London and the Massachusetts Institute of Technology. No surprises there.

Canada does snag spot #19 with McGill University (which is a much higher spot than Canada's best museum managed to score.) As well, Canada was only one of three countries other than the US and UK to have universities ranked in the top twenty (Switzerland grabbed #18 and Australia #20). The University of Toronto (#29), the University of British Columbia (#44), and the University of Alberta (#78) also make the top 100.

Also ranked in the Top 400 are Queen's University (#132), Université de Montréal (#136), University of Waterloo (#145), McMaster University (#162), Western Ontario (#164), University of Calgary (#165), Dalhousie (#212), Simon Fraser (#214), University of Ottawa (#231), University of Victoria (#241), Laval University (#271), York (#333), University of Manitoba (#357). (Carleton, Concordia, and Université du Québec are also listed but not ranked.)

All in all, Canada has 20 Universities in the top 642 schools in the world that were ranked, or about 3.1%. Considering that Canada's population accounts for only 0.5% of the world's total population, we appear to be doing quite well when it comes to globally recognized universities. However, if you compare Canada to other countries with roughly the same level of wealth and economic well-being, the ratio of good schools to population in Canada is much less favourable. With this in perspective, 3% of the world's top universities is only so-so.

America's Greatest Friend?

Another example of where Canada ranks in the eyes of the world—and in fact the eyes of its closest neighbour and largest trading partner—comes from a speech given by President George W. Bush before a Joint Session of Congress on September 20, 2001. America was just recovering from the shock and terror of the 9/11 attack. The eyes and the ears of the world were on the US as the President went out of his way to thank and praise countries around the world for their actions and support:

> And on behalf of the American people, I thank the world for its outpouring of support. America will never forget the sounds of our national anthem playing at Buckingham Palace, on the streets of Paris and at Berlin's Brandenburg Gate. We will not forget South Korean children gathering to pray outside our embassy in Seoul, or the prayers of sympathy offered at a mosque in Cairo. We will not forget moments of silence and days of mourning in Australia and Africa and Latin America. Nor will we forget the citizens of 80 other nations who died with our own. Dozens of Pakistanis, more than 130 Israelis, more than 250 citizens of India, men and women from El Salvador, Iran, Mexico and Japan, and hundreds of British citizens. America has no truer friend than Great Britain.[28]

Countries mentioned included Iran, Egypt, France and Pakistan—hardly a list of George Dubya's buddies. Neighbouring Mexico was mentioned as well, despite the fact that the US is building an actual fence to keep Mexicans out of the country. Nods were handed out to small countries like Korea, Australia and Israel.

Canada, on the other hand, didn't receive so much as a passing reference in the speech. No thanks paid for being the country most involved in assisting stranded American travelers who could not get home for days due to the stoppage of air travel. Not even a verbal acknowledgement of the 24 Canadians killed in the World Trade Centre attack, which must have been higher than the number of El Salvadorians.

And the kicker? "America has no truer friend than *Great Britain*." That sentence should have ended with *Canada* given the two nations' close economic, political and cultural ties. Wasn't the US born from struggle and rebellion against Great Britain? Canada, on the other hand, was shut out. Completely unacknowledged.

Many would suggest a speech given by the unpopular Bush Jr. shouldn't be taken too seriously, but he was the President of the United States, and at that point in history, the most powerful and influential man on the planet. This was an important speech planned and written well in advance, not an off-the-cuff media briefing. It was well-thought out. And his not mentioning Canada in this speech was noticed by Canadians. But was this slight noticed by anyone else in the world? Probably not.

Sometimes, though, Canada has received international attention, although not always the best kind. In transcripts of a speech in November 2002, Osama bin Laden threatened Britain, France, Italy, Germany, Australia and Canada for their support for the United States, saying: "It is time that we get even. You will be killed just as you kill, and will be bombed just as you bomb."[29] It was nice to be recognized, but in this case a little less recognition would have been preferred. However, Canada has yet to experience any direct terrorist attacks from al-Qaeda, while many of these others have. In this case, perhaps being low profile is a blessing?

Going from Invisible to Indispensible

The magazines, online surveys, and lists mentioned in this chapter do not constitute definitive evidence about how much the world thinks about Canada. Nonetheless, they suggest that Canada is not top of mind around the world. Whether it is economic prowess, educational options, the arts or many other areas of endeavour, Canada is not generally thought of as a global leader. Canada is not *totally* invisible, but it is not the household name it needs to be in order to compete at the highest levels of the international economy. As noted, there are exceptions. For example, Canada has been praised for not letting its banks run amok as they have in many other places. This is nice to hear, but it is not the kind of wow factor Canada needs.

We want to emphasize that the purpose of highlighting Canada's relative invisibility is not to belittle or downgrade Canada in any way. We think Canada is a fantastic country with all kinds of great things happening and with the potential to do much more. We would not be writing this book if we didn't believe that Canada is capable of world-class accomplishments. We also hope that this chapter doesn't sound whiney. Rather, we present these sources to make the point that, in the eyes of the rest of the world, Canada is underrated. The global community doesn't know enough about Canada. This is a problem, because reputation, backed by substance and the ability to deliver, matter in the international economic arena.

In the next chapter we explore some of the reasons why Canada's profile is so low and why this poses an economic problem.

Chapter 5

How Do I Look? Why Profile Matters in the International Economy

> "You wouldn't think of building an NHL team without scouting for the world's best people. I don't see why we would think of building a world-class knowledge economy without having the world's best people."
> —Professor Arvind Gupta, CEO and Director of MITACS Inc.

Let's review the information presented in Chapter 4 which painted a picture of Canada's international profile. How much attention does the world pay to Canada?

→ In the global media (as measured by mentions in *The Economist* magazine), Canada is represented far less than its G7 peers; however, in relation to the size of its economy and population, Canada holds its own—barely.

→ On lists of liveable cities, Canada does very well. So at least the world recognizes that Canada has cities that offer a high quality of life.

→ In terms of "great" cities as measured by influence, economic power and knowledge, Canada fares rather poorly—only Toronto gets mentioned in the global Top 40 and it falls out of the expected rankings altogether ten years from now.

→ In arts, culture and design, Canada is completely left in the dust.

→ Canada's post-secondary education is reasonably well recognized, but compared to countries of similar living standards and wealth, its profile is mediocre.

→ George Bush left Canada out of a key speech and apparently America has "no truer friend" than Great Britain.

Although there is no handy empirical confirmation of this, it is safe to say that the following phrases do *not* generally come to mind when people think of Canada: "economic powerhouse," "business acumen," "world leader," "cutting edge" and "creative hotspot." Whether Canada's low profile is the result of the world not noticing Canada or because Canadians are not making themselves noticed, it's a problem because the old adage "it's not what you know but who you know" applies to the Canadian economy just as it does to job seekers.

Are Things Changing?

It's not all bad news for Canada. There have been some developments over the past five years or so that suggest Canada's international profile has indeed been rising.

After the Vancouver 2010 Olympic Winter Games, some suggested that Canada reached a turning point. Not only did Canada show the world that its athletes can compete with the best in the world (something that had been questioned in previous Olympic outings), but that they could dominate: Canadian athletes won more gold medals than any other country had ever managed to do at the winter games. Canadians also showed the world an outpouring of national pride in the streets of Vancouver during those two weeks—a joyful, spontaneous love of country that would rival displays of patriotism anywhere in the world. Canadians proved to themselves that they are world class and worthy of international attention. And it seemed that no one was more surprised by Canada's athletic performance and national pride than Canadians themselves.

Canada's solid economic performance through the downturn of the 2008-09 recession did not go unnoticed by the rest of the world. In 2008, in the pit of the financial crisis when banks around the globe were going belly-up, the World Economic Forum recognized Canadian banks as the most stable and well-capitalized in the world. In this case, Canada's more conservative lending practices saved it from the horrible fates of other countries where banks and lenders were badly overleveraged. The Federal Finance Minister Jim Flahrety was awarded "Finance Minister of the Year" by the respected *Euromoney* magazine in 2009.[30] And *Time* magazine recognized Bank of Canada Governor Mark Carney as one of the top 100 most influential people in 2010.[31] In late 2011, Mr. Carney was appointed to head up the G20's Financial Stability Board, a highly influential and globally significant position.

Canada's energy sector is another factor that has gained us the attention of the world—but for both positive and negative reasons. On the positive side, Canada is increasingly being recognized as a significant player in crude oil supply. (Prime Minister Harper has described Canada as an energy "superpower" but that may yet be a bit of a stretch in the eyes of the rest of the world. Most Americans have absolutely no idea that Canada is their largest supplier of energy.) Canada's wealth of natural resources have been noticed by the international business community, particularly in China. And international investment bankers are setting up shop in places like Calgary to help finance some very large deals as global companies scramble for a piece of Canada's bitumen wealth.

But the misinformation and bad publicity around Alberta's oil sands has delivered some very negative attention in global circles, especially among environmentalists. At the UN Climate Change Conferences in both Copenhagen and Cancun, Canada was awarded multiple "Fossil Awards" by the Climate Action Network (an international consortium of roughly 500 environmental organizations). While few take the "Fossil Award" seriously, it's still not the kind of attention Canada would like.

Aside from some of the negative press, these recent developments are encouraging. Canada is starting to show some long overdue moxie in global affairs. But while it's a good start, Canada still has to do much more in the coming years to raise its international profile.

Why Does International Profile Matter?

Some may argue that Canada's low profile internationally does not make one bit of difference to its future economic performance. Some may go so far as to suggest that a low profile is an advantage. Why attract attention to ourselves? What matters is that Canada has the natural resources that the world needs and that it has the world's largest economy on its doorstep. Who cares if George Bush didn't mention Canada in some dumb speech? All of this nonsense about Canada getting mentioned in books about graphic designers, being ranked among the great cities and having fancy museums is completely irrelevant information.

Nothing could be further from the truth.

The Case of India

Just prior to the International Indian Film Academy (IIFA) awards being held in Toronto in June of 2011, Indo-Canadian journalist and reporter Faiz Jamil prepared a piece for the CBC website. The essay focuses on the awareness that contemporary Indians have of Canada—even with us hosting the IIFA awards.

Jamil sums it up: "We simply don't register."[32]

> Not even the fact that the IIFA awards are being handed out in Toronto—the first time the huge ceremony has been in North America—seems to be generating much curiosity about Canada, either in the media or the public's mind. That these awards are often called the "Bollywood Oscars" pretty much gives away which western country has most of India's attention. This tends to be followed by the old colonial master, Britain, and then Australia, where many smart young Indians go if they are looking for an affordable western education.

Canada, at least in the minds of India's best, brightest and most creative, tends to be an afterthought. "The Lokhandwala area of Mumbai is home to many artists, producers and other workers in India's film industry. Mention Canada here and you'll get responses ranging from 'beautiful country' to 'very friendly people,'" writes Jamil.

Beautiful and friendly is a good start, but clearly Canada is not keeping pace in attracting the best and brightest minds from around the world—including millions of young people in India—as the place in which they want to study, learn or set up a business.

Arvind Gupta is the CEO and scientific director of MITACS Inc., a national research network that builds connections between industry and Canadian universities. In an interview with the *Globe and Mail* in 2010, Mr. Gupta describes how Canadian schools are not in the sights of the best students in India. According to him, India's top students with the highest grade point averages head to Stanford or Princeton.

Australia has been more aggressive in its recruitment efforts in recent years, which has put schools in that country in the second tier of preferred study destinations. This has been matched by recruiting programs in Britain, France and Germany.

Canada is the destination of the students with grades too low to get into the better schools in the US, Australia or Europe. "These kids are not knocking on our door," says Prof. Gupta, who is also a Computer Science Professor at the University of British Columbia. "They've got Princeton and Stanford going to recruit them. They've got options. The whole world is coming after talent."[33]

It's not as though Canada has been idly standing by watching this happen, though. There have been some pretty serious efforts on the part of governments to reverse this trend and start attracting international brain power. For example, 19 Canada Excellence Research Chairs, each worth $10 million over seven years, were created by the federal government to boost academic excellence and attract star international researchers. There has also been the 70 Banting Postdoctoral Fellowships, each worth $70,000 a year for two years, also put in place by Ottawa. The government of Ontario has instituted four-year, $45,000-a-year scholarships for foreign PhD researchers, and the Perimeter Institute in Waterloo, Ontario has set up five research chairs in theoretical physics.

These efforts are helping, but more needs to be done—and not just by governments, either.

Time to Stop Being a Wallflower

On the international stage, Canada needs to raise its profile and not be so timid. It needs to shake off its collective inferiority complex that it has carried around for so long (perhaps an unfortunate side effect of having grown up beside such a large and accomplished neighbour to the south). Canadians need to be proud, not boastful. Ambitious, not arrogant. Confident, not cocky. They need to stand up and be recognized. Canada's international profile needs a big boost, but it has to be earned, not demanded.

In a small and shrinking global economy, exposure is vital. Canada is in a fierce competition not only for marketing its cars, lumber and oil, but also for scarce international capital. Canada competes for international students and artists looking for universities. It competes for global tourists seeking modern, cosmopolitan cities with great art and culture. It competes for business people looking for great market opportunities.

Are global capital managers, students, artists, tourists and entrepreneurs thinking about Canada? Will the best and brightest in the world beat a path to Canada's door to fulfill their economic dreams? Can young Canadians find enough reasons to return to their home country while they pursue careers in art, design, technology and education? They won't if Canada continues to be so invisible on the global stage. Canada and Canadians need to be indispensible, not invisible.

Canadians will get noticed if they are doing interesting, creative and innovative things and if they are not shy about being Canadian. It's not just a pride issue, it's an economic issue.

Epilogue to Part A

In the preceding five chapters, we've described the situation in which the Canadian economy finds itself in the second decade of the 21st century. Unfortunately, it doesn't look so good.

Like the metaphor of the frog in the pot of water, Canada has done nothing particularly wrong—indeed, it has done a lot of things right. Canada would not be among the world's most desirable places to live, nor would its economy have survived the global recession of 2008-09 as well as it did, if it had being doing everything wrong.

But also like that frog in the pot of heating water, Canada's economic environment is changing—and changing quickly. The water in the pot is getting uncomfortably hot; the time has come to take some determined, intentional steps to jump out.

In Chapter 1, it was argued that traditional manufacturing in Canada has long ago turned a corner. Because of the rise of the emerging economies and their lower costs of production (especially labour), Canada cannot anticipate a return to its glory days of mass manufacturing, no matter what kind of tax credits or government carrots are offered. Manufacturing still has a future in Canada, but it will require some major changes in scope and attitude.

Chapter 2 made the case that natural resource economics have changed, too. Despite being incredibly blessed with almost every kind of resource the world needs, it is a fool's paradise to believe Canada can blithely keep extracting oil, trees, metals and crops in the same way in which it has done it for the past century. The pressure is on Canada to improve its environmental record, as well as its economic competitiveness. Natural resources have a bright future in Canada, but they can't drive the economy all on their own.

Chapter 3 described how the global economy has become much more intertwined and connected. Canada's place in that tightly woven web is not assured, and it's up to Canadians to find their own niche in the rapidly evolving—but much more nuanced—chain of production.

Chapter 4 made the case that despite the rest of the world thinking Canada is pretty swell, they really don't give it much thought at all. Canada is often ignored, invisible, underrated—and if Canadians want global attention and recognition (and the economic opportunities they bring), they are going to have to work harder to earn them. Canadians need to get better at selling themselves.

Chapter 5 concluded Part A by arguing that Canada's lack of global prominence is preventing it from attracting the best and brightest the world has to offer.

We're not the only ones suggesting Canada is facing a challenge, either. In a 2011 report by Deloitte Canada entitled "The Future of Productivity," authors Bill Currie, Larry Scott and Alain Coté describe the decreasing competitive advantage currency engulfing the Canadian economy. Many of their five main areas of concern are reflected in Part A of this book (see Figure 2).

FIGURE 2: Canada's Decreasing Competitive Advantages[34]

	Past	Present
Demographics	Canada's labour force was growing as a percentage of the population; hours worked per employee was on the rise	An aging population is increasing the proportion of retirees and reducing hours worked
Canadian dollar	A low Canadian dollar created a price advantage, reducing other competitive pressures	A falling US dollar is eroding Canada's price advantage
Access to US markets	The signing of the NAFTA in 1992 gave Canada unrivalled access to the US markets	Canada's share of US imports is declining while the importance of non-US markets is growing
Global marketplace	The global marketplace was dominated by mature economies with similar labour costs	The emergence of developing economies has heightened global competition and increased availability of lower-cost substitutes
Commodity extraction	Strong demand for commodities drove growth in Canadian resource extraction and depleted the most accessible reserves	Resource companies are now forced to explore less productive reserves such as the oil sands

Canadians generally feel pretty good about their country, and they've had some reasons to smile in the last few years. Notably, the Vancouver 2010 Olympic Winter Games provided a huge patriotic morale boost. But, despite all they've done right, many Canadians have a feeling that they could be doing better. There is a niggling worry out there that Canada is not fully living up to its potential. And we couldn't agree more.

We believe Canada has the potential to regain competitiveness, boost productivity, attract the best and brightest workers in the world, and gain the respect and recognition of the global economy. We believe Canada can be a global leader in raising living standards, improving economic outcomes, protecting the natural environment in which we live and helping to forge a better future for the world.

How is Canada going to achieve all of this? We believe Canada has the potential to transform its economy through the *generation and implementation of great ideas*. Like the frog in the pot of water, Canada's world is changing. The water is heating up. Not only does Canada need to figure a way out of the pot, it needs to rewrite its economic DNA so it can survive in the world beyond it.

Canada's frog-in-the-pot-of-water moment has arrived. Part B explains how Canada can jump out and thrive in a new world.

Part B

The Solution → A New Economic DNA for Canada

Chapter 6

Unleashing Creativity

"My contention is that creativity now is as important in education as literacy, and we should treat it with the same status."
— Sir Ken Robinson[35]

"We consistently fail to grasp how many ideas remain to be discovered. ... Possibilities do not add up. They multiply."
— Paul Romer[36]

The Creativity Riddle

Over the past several years, economists and politicians in North America have linked economic growth and creativity. Management gurus and business schools wax on about the imperatives of innovation and creativity. Entire volumes have been written on how the future belongs to countries, cities and communities with creative workers.

But is the word "creativity" staring to lose its meaning?

In February 2009, as part of a project at the Martin Prosperity Institute at the University of Toronto, Richard Florida and Roger Martin—two of Canada's top minds on the subject of creativity in the economy—delivered a report called *Ontario in the Creative Age*.[37] The report was commissioned by Premier McGuinty's government as a way of kick-starting a new conversation about where the Ontario (and Canadian) economy could succeed in a world that has radically changed.

The report was top-notch. But when commenting on Florida's and Martin's urging for more creativity in routine-oriented jobs, Premier McGuinty said: "I don't know exactly what that means."[38] This sums up the problem. A lot of very smart people—including folks like Roger Martin and even the Premier of Ontario—have bought into the whole idea of fostering creativity in the economy. But at the root of it, most of us might agree with Mr. McGuinty and admit we don't know exactly what that means.

Creativity has become a flash word, one that flies around corporate boardroom tables, government sponsored reports and MBA group presentations. It gets nods of agreement and easily deflects any dissention. Who could possibly suggest that the economy needs *less* creativity? The word itself is full of meaning, but unfortunately it is dangerously close to becoming like other overused words and phrases that business management wonks have beaten to death such as "think outside the box" and "paradigm shift."

Sadly, the word creativity is becoming jargon. Any discussion of the importance of creativity in the economy risks mimicking all of the other volumes of books and reports out there calling for more creative workers. As much as we would like to, we can't dump the word creative. Beneath the jargon-filled baggage economists and sociologists have heaped on it, it conveys a particular notion distinct from being smart, clever, knowledgeable, or even wise.

What does creative really mean? According to the *Oxford Canadian Dictionary*, creative is an adjective that means:

1) of or involving the skilful and imaginative use of something to produce e.g., a work of art

2) able to create things, usually in an imaginative way

3) inventive.

Other thinkers and writers on the subject of creativity give more colour and depth to the definition of creativity. Linda Naiman, the Vancouver-based founder of Creativity at Work, is a creativity and innovation consultant, coach, speaker and author. She is recognized internationally for pioneering arts-based learning as a catalyst for developing creativity, innovation, and collaborative leadership in organizations. She defines creativity this way: "creativity [is] the act of turning new and imaginative ideas into reality. Creativity involves two processes: thinking, then producing. If you have ideas, but don't act on them, you are imaginative but not creative."[39]

On her website, Naiman cites other definitions of creativity that bring even more light to the subject:

> Creativity is the process of bringing something new into being...creativity requires passion and commitment. Out of the creative act is born symbols and myths. It brings to our awareness what was previously hidden and points to new life. The experience is one of heightened consciousness-ecstasy.[40]

> A product is creative when it is (a) novel and (b) appropriate. A novel product is original not predictable. The bigger the concept, and the more the product stimulates further work and ideas, the more the product is creative.[41]

These definitions reveal three consistent themes regarding creativity: newness, originality and action.

A Better Recipe

American economist Paul Romer has a distinguished *curriculum vitae*. He is a Senior Fellow at Stanford University's Center for International Development and the Stanford Institute for Economic Policy Research and a Non-Resident Fellow at the Center for Global Development. Romer is an expert on economic growth and is credited with the witty quotation "A crisis is a terrible thing to waste." But Romer is also an expert on how creativity and ideas are an essential ingredient in the economy:

> Economic growth occurs whenever people take resources and rearrange them in ways that are more valuable. A useful metaphor for production in an economy comes from the kitchen. To create valuable final products, we mix inexpensive ingredients together according to a recipe. The cooking one can do is limited by the supply of ingredients, and most cooking in the economy produces undesirable side effects. If economic growth could be achieved only by doing more and more of the same kind of cooking, we would eventually run out of raw materials and suffer from unacceptable levels of pollution and nuisance. History teaches us, however, that economic growth springs from better recipes, not just from more cooking. New recipes generally produce fewer unpleasant side effects and generate more economic value per unit of raw material.
>
> Every generation has perceived the limits to growth that finite resources and undesirable side effects would pose if no new recipes or ideas were discovered. And every generation has underestimated the potential for finding new recipes and ideas. We consistently fail to grasp how many ideas remain to be discovered. Possibilities do not add up. They multiply.[42]

But as wonderful as the economics of new ideas are, Romer also offers a warning:

> Leading countries like the United States, Canada, and the members of the European Union cannot stay ahead merely by adopting ideas developed elsewhere. They must offer strong incentives for discovering new ideas at home, and this is not easy to do. The same characteristic that makes an idea so valuable—everybody can use it at the same time—also means that it is hard to earn an appropriate rate of return on investments in ideas. The many people who benefit from a new idea can too easily free ride on the efforts of others.[43]

Clearly, from an economist's perspective, new ideas are the essential backbone of the modern economy. And it is out of creativity that new ideas—and wealth—are born.

A Valuable Proposition

Renowned educator and lecturer Sir Ken Robinson offers his own definition of creativity, one that is the simplest and therefore perhaps the most useful: "my definition of creativity is this: imaginative processes with outcomes that are original and of value."[44] Accepting Robinson's definition, then, requires that we explore the meaning of the word "value." What is value? And how can an original idea have value?

Typically, economists like to associate value with a market price. The value of a car or a barrel of oil is usually defined as the dollar price a seller could expect to receive for its sale. Sometimes, if the market is not quite as robust as a seller would like (think of a slow market for real estate), the seller may not agree with the price he or she could get, contending that the item is "more valuable" than that, even if the market price says it isn't. But in both cases, the "value" of something is set relative to the market price signals.

But there are other cases in which the market price is almost irrelevant to value. Value also has to do with usefulness and immediacy. For most Canadian drivers in the winter, an ice scraper is an extremely valuable and useful tool for those mornings when the windshield has frosted over—yet the market price of a small, plastic ice scraper would not suggest it is very valuable. Or, how many of us have ever needed a tissue for a runny nose? Even though a tissue is almost valueless (maybe a couple of dollars to buy a box of a hundred or more), in the immediacy of the moment, value changes.

Unique situations can also dictate the value of certain items. The market price of diamonds implies that they are extremely valuable, and indeed people will pay dearly for the beauty and luxury of diamond jewelry. But if stranded on a desert island with no provisions, a glass of drinkable water is suddenly infinitely more valuable than a diamond ring.

And often great value is attached to items with no usefulness at all—at least no usefulness yet. When asked about the usefulness of his discovery of electricity, Michael Faraday quipped: "What use is a baby?" Yet a baby is typically treasured above everything else by its parents. There is obviously an emotional value that a parent puts on a child, driven by our biological instincts. It's silly to even suggest we try to determine the value of a baby. Great artwork, antiques, and spectacular natural vistas are other examples of things with little use, but of extraordinary value. They are irreplaceable, and once they're gone, they're gone forever.

Returning to Robinson's definition of creativity, how can an original idea possess value? The processes of *invention, innovation, and design* are the stepping stones in creating value—new products and services which hold the potential to improve social wellbeing and add to the economy. Each process is unique, but each holds the capacity to create value for the originator. Obviously, market signals and prices can come into play with creative ideas, particularly ones that can be turned into a consumer product and sold for a profit. A creative idea for a new product or service, for example, is dead in the water around the boardroom table if there is no way it can be commercialized.

Invention, Innovation and Design

There are several different ways to think about invention, innovation and design, and certainly many writers and thinkers on this subject have offered up their own unique (and sometimes contradictory) definitions. But for the purposes of this chapter, the following basic definitions are offered.

Invention is the *process of creating something new and unique*. The combustion engine, the microprocessor, and the electric light bulb are good examples of true inventions. At this stage, there does not necessarily have to be a practical application of the invention. True invention is quite rare.

Innovation can be described as *the application of an existing technology to a new and very useful purpose*. Examples of innovations are the modern automobile (the application of the combustion engine to transportation), digital music (the application of the microprocessor to digitize information) and street lamps (the application of electric light to make roads safer). Notice the difference between invention and innovation: the former is something brand new, while the latter is really just taking the invention and finding a new, practical use for it.

Design is the *improvement of an existing technology to create a more practical, more useful, or more aesthetically pleasing item*. The Apple iPod is a perfect example of great design. Note that the iPod was not the introduction of the microprocessor (the invention stage), nor was it the first portable digital music player (the innovation stage). Rather, it was an ingenious series of improvements to how the portable digital audio player worked and interfaced with the user.

In practice, invention, innovation and design often play off one another in the creative process. Nonetheless, these categories are useful for understanding how each snakes through the development of new products.

There is a fourth level of product development that could be called "enhanced product variety." A chewing gum company that comes up with a new flavor with an enticing name like *Ice Chiller* or *Tropical Explosion* is enhancing consumer selection and hoping to gain a fraction of the market in the process. But while creativity is involved, it should not be confused with invention, innovation or design. This is a mistake many companies make: they think of themselves as innovative, but coming up with a new and unique flavor of chewing gum alone is not true innovation.

Thinking beyond the profit-motivated companies that form the backbone of the market economy, creativity generates unique ideas with value in other areas, too. Many of the inventions, innovations and designs in the world of science and academia were driven not by profits, but by naturally inquisitive minds. Think of the invention of the telescope, of modern mathematics and of penicillin—all extremely valuable in improving the world for humankind, but none driven by a boardroom's demand for higher quarterly profits.

As well, many of the most useful and valuable technological developments have been the result of human collaboration seeking a solution to a problem. The Internet, the modern accounting system, and GPS technologies are good examples. Profits have been made because of all three, but profit was not the primary motivating factor in their development.

Creativity Ahead of its Time

Judging the value of new ideas can be difficult. By definition, creative ideas are often ahead of their times. In the mid-1830s, Michael Faraday gave the first demonstrations of electricity at the Royal Institution in London. He stood in a gaslit lecture threatre before a distinguished audience of scientists and showed bright blue sparks leaping between two copper spheres. The audience was impressed, but many of them were at a loss to know what to make of it all. 'This is all very interesting, Mr Faraday', said one of them. 'But what use is it?' 'I don't know,' said Faraday, 'what use is a baby?' A world without electricity is now unthinkable. Our lives depend on it in almost every way, from food supplies to transport to heating, lighting and telecommunications. The 19th century had none of the uses of electricity that we now take for granted. It was not that people had their homes cluttered with dishwashers and televisions simply waiting for Faraday to complete his experiments. The applications of electricity only followed the harnessing of electricity itself. Faraday's discoveries created circumstances in which the applications were developed. At the time, many people simply couldn't see the point of it. This is often the way with creative insights. They run ahead of their times and confuse the crowd.

– Ken Robinson, *Out of Our Minds: Learning to be Creative*

Creativity is the Common Thread

Creativity, then, adds value to society and the economy through the distinct processes of invention, innovation and design. All three of these processes are unique, all require creativity, and all hold the potential to help improve economic conditions and opportunities for humankind. So if we accept that creativity is essential to the economy, and that invention, innovation and design add value, the next questions to ask are: How do we foster a culture of creativity? Where does creativity come from?

Teach Your Children Well

Canada's K-12 primary and secondary education system is actually quite good, at least as judged by the most recent round of the OECD's *Programme for International Student Assessment* (PISA), an internationally standardized assessment of student performance jointly developed by participating OECD countries and administered to 15-year-olds in schools around the world.[45] In the 2009 round of exams, Canadian students ranked 6th in reading, 10th in math, and 8th in science (ranked out of 65 participating countries in the PISA survey, which includes all 34 OECD countries). Although being 1st would be the ultimate goal, a solid "top ten" finish is quite respectable and attests to the quality of education in Canada.

But are Canadian students creative? Clever kids aren't the ones who simply memorize information; clever kids are the ones who *learn how to learn*. That is something for which the PISA scores do not offer much insight. In much of the thinking on economic competitiveness, there tends to be an emphasis on education in science, math and applied technical skills. Without question, these are essential if Canada's economy has any chance of success in the coming years.

But a test tube can solve no problems. A hammer can build nothing. And even the most powerful computer can't create anything. What each of them needs is a human brain to operate them in order to solve, build and create. Obviously, knowing how to use a test tube, a hammer and a computer is essential, but what Canada needs now more than ever is clever ideas for using them to solve 21st century problems. We don't need a Fountain of Youth; we need a Fountain of *Creativity*.

A few years ago, Daniel Pink authored a book entitled *A Whole New Mind*.[46] He argued that linear-thinking and "left brain" occupations such as medicine, engineering and computer science contributed significantly to our economic wealth in the 20th century. But increasingly, because of competition from Asia and the advances in computing ability, what Canadian workers really need in the 21st century are more "right brain" attributes—skills such as imagination, intuition, story telling, play, empathy and relational abilities—to complement their linear thinking. Pink argues that the right brain attributes are just as essential as the left brain attributes, but that it is not really one or the other—it is both sides of the brain working together that generates creative ideas. It is, in his words, a whole new mind.

How do we foster creativity? When it comes to our children, the answer is almost comically simple: stop pounding the creativity out of them. The education system in Canada was designed to discourage creativity, inventiveness and originality. Thankfully, huge strides are being made by some of Canada's most thoughtful education practitioners to correct this.

One example of how to foster inventiveness and originality in children is found at the Calgary Arts Academy. This K-9 charter school is not an arts school; rather, it's an arts *immersion* school that delivers the standard Alberta curriculum through art. At the Calgary Arts Academy, teachers work alongside artists to design the program. Kids learn math through music and dance, for example, or social studies through drama. Instead of making the kids read about and memorize types of cloud formations, they get them to write a play and act like clouds. By doing so, they engage their whole brain in learning the defining characteristics of different cloud types. And by engaging their whole brains, they become what Canada needs them to be: creative, clever and ready to take on a rapidly changing 21st century.

A Revolution in Education

Recently, teachers of a young grade 4 student in a typical public school noticed something unusual about the boy. He would be singing and drumming out rhythms all the time, naturally and without inhibition. They decided to call a meeting with his parents.

"Your son has music running through his head at all times," they told the parents, who had also noted his musical proclivities. The parents beamed.

Then the teachers said flatly, "This has GOT to stop!" The parents were shocked. Rather than recognizing the boy's special abilities and characteristics as a gift to be fostered, the teachers regarded the music and rhythms running through his head as a nuisance. In some ways, you can understand the teachers' point. The boy's musical tendency probably was a distraction to the traditional classroom setting. It probably did get in the teachers' way. But rather than find a way to channel his abilities as a part of his learning experience, the teachers thought it best if the music stopped.

Fortunately, the boy's parents did not see it that way. They moved their child to the Calgary Arts Academy, where students learn the regular provincial curriculum through art: the boy is learning math through rhythms and music. His gift is now an asset to his learning, rather than something to be crushed.

It is important to note that teachers are not to blame in these situations. The problem lies at a systemic level. What Canada needs is a radical rethinking of its education system. The current system is good, but it is not *good enough* at recognizing and maximizing the creativity and special gifts children bring with them to school.

Taking Action

Most of us who have ever spent any time at all around children know how naturally creative they can be. The art of imagination during playtime is, sadly, something that is lost on most adults as we busy ourselves with more "serious" academic pursuits in school and the work world that lies beyond. People say all the time, "Oh, I'm not creative." But in fact, everyone is creative, or at least has the potential to be. Most of us have no idea of the creative capacity we possess and this represents an enormous loss.

A creative person is one who purposely tries to look at a problem or a situation in a new way. Creativity is not a genetic trait, like having brown hair or blue eyes. It is an ability each of us has at childhood, but is too often forgotten in adulthood. According to Robinson: "Creativity is not a separate faculty that some people have and others do not. It is a function of intelligence: it takes many forms, it draws from many different capacities and we all have different creative capacities. Creativity is possible in any activity in which human intelligence is activity engaged."[47]

In *Out of Our Minds,* Robinson provides a detailed description of the human capacities and abilities for two related—yet different—mental processes: imagination and creativity.

Imagination is the ability to visualize or conceptualize something that is not actually right in front of you. Imagination means seeing "in the mind's eye."[48] It can be of something familiar, such as if you were asked to imagine a sunset. But it is also possible to imagine things completely nonsensical, with no personal experience on which to draw. Robinson, for example, asks his readers to imagine a green polar bear wearing a dress. This is possible because of the human mind's mental capacity to imagine.

Creativity, however, is different from imagination:

> Private imaginings may have no impact on the public world at all. Creativity does. It would be odd to describe someone as creative who just lay still and never did anything. Whatever the task, creativity is not just an internal mental process: it involves action. In a sense, it is applied imagination. To call somebody creative suggests they are actively producing something in a deliberate way.

> [One of the things to] recognize is that being creative involves doing something. People are not creative in the abstract; they are creative in something—in mathematics, in engineering, in writing, in music, in business, in whatever. You could not be creative unless you were actually doing something. In this respect, creativity is different from imagination.[49]

The implication of this is that, to actually be creative, you have to get off your butt and do something. The outcomes of the first few steps are not as important as the actual action of taking them. So, one of the traits of a creative person is the willingness to take action on an idea, an impulse or a hunch.

Creative Workers

All of us are creative and exercising that creativity is an economic imperative. There is not a single sector of the economy that would not benefit from clever solutions to problems, new ways of seeing things and unique products. Creative workers are those who find solutions to the problems they encounter on the job, but here we need an increased effort from both employers and employees.

Certainly there are many who will quickly dismiss this as a waste of time and money. And when companies have to make tough budget choices, it's almost a certainty that team building days and offsite activities to boost creativity (especially if the activity is the least bit fun or enjoyable) are the first things to go. Sadly, creativity is still considered a superfluous, nice-to-have-but-not-essential part of workplace training. And even worse are those managers and employees who are hostile toward creativity-building exercises: not only do they think it's a waste of time, they think that it's a *stupid* waste of time.

These attitudes need to change. Canadian companies, managers, employees, and self-employed individuals need to recognize that creative thinking is not some airy-fairy pastime only for poets and artists (i.e., in the minds of some, those people who do not add anything of value to the economy). But activating all parts of the human brain is no silly diversion, and it could do amazing things to help Canadians work more productively, get more enjoyment out of their jobs, and find clever solutions to the problems they encounter in the workplace.

And things *are* starting to change. A growing movement within the corporate world lies in the seemingly odd marriage of art and design with business acumen and bottom-line pragmatism. What's been lacking up until now is the understanding of how to merge art and business and see what comes falling out from the creative friction that develops. For example, if you collect a group of accountants in a room and ask them to solve some sort of problem, there will be solutions offered up—and many of them might well be quite good solutions. But generally, the accountants will all approach the problem from the same perspective. This can be severely limiting for companies that are looking for innovative, creative solutions. But drop, say, a photography student or a classically trained musician into the mix. Take someone from a totally different educational background and ask them to participate in solving some sort of problem. (Despite the obvious fact that the photographer or musician may not understand the language and technical aspects of accounting, this can be overcome if everyone buys into the exercise.) It's almost like the high school chemistry experiments where a small drop of some element or chemical is dropped into a stable solution of some other chemical: the introduction of something new into something old can really generate quite a reaction.

The reality is that both the accountants and the artists are problem solvers. They are all attempting to take an existing situation—be it a financial ledger, a blank palate, or an unresolved orchestral movement—and create something of value from it. Financial wizards and artists are not worlds apart after all. They're all trying to do one thing: solve a problem.

This isn't to guilt businesses into hiring artists with no apparent skill or background in the sector, although the benefits of this may indeed be surprising. Rather, Canadians should stop thinking about arts (and the creativity they can generate) as superfluous "nice-to-haves." They are essential elements for business, for society and for the economy. And they are essential not because of the GDP generated by artists and their work (which is the usual defense artists offer up). They are essential because they hold the potential to transform our minds and stimulate creativity. The point is not a trivial one.

Using Technology to Spark Creativity

Traditionally, companies thought they were doing quite well in engaging their workers and tapping into their creative ideas with the "Suggestion Box." The suggestions were independent, static messages scrawled on a piece of paper and shoved into a box, left for days (weeks?) until they were read by someone in some position of authority. And when that person did read them, the fate of the idea or suggestion rested entirely with how it was received by that single reader; if he or she didn't think the idea had merit, it probably died right then and there.

But today's electronic technologies allow for fluid, dynamic, and interactive "Idea Forums." Employees are encouraged to post ideas for making the workplace better, more productive, etc. They can even suggest new products or enhanced designs for existing ones. Because everyone else in the company can read the posts, a dialogue begins. The idea may or may not be a great one to start with, but the possibility exists for others to build on the idea and turn it into a truly fantastic one.

Of course, encouraging workers to "be creative" and engage in some sort of online idea forum comes with certain perils for the company. Static ideas shoved into the traditional suggestion box can be easily ignored. But asking workers to participate in a discussion could result in some ideas—be they good or bad—that are more difficult to deal with. Ignoring them may not be an option. Someone may suggest giving employees every Friday off as a morale booster, but explaining to them why that's not going to happen may actually *reduce* morale. Genuinely asking employees for ideas and suggestions holds the potential for opening a Pandora's Box.

Here's where management needs to be proactive with their electronic forums. Put the onus on the suggestion-maker by asking them to explain how the idea meets criteria: Will it improve profitability or efficiency? Will it improve workplace safety? Will worker engagement and retention improve? etc. If the idea does manage to meet these, then perhaps it's a good idea. It may even be a *great* idea.

All of this requires some investment on the part of management. Setting up an electronic idea forum for workers will do no good—and in fact, it could do more harm—if it is ignored. Yet this sort of activity offers tremendous potential to stir creativity and generate new ideas.

Time for Creative Thought

A trend noticed in some of the world's most cutting-edge companies (especially high-tech ones in which new, creative ideas are as good as gold) is to give employees time at work to spend on their own creative pursuits. Google has been notable on this front, with its "20% time" as a workplace philosophy. The idea is to give workers one day a week on the company's dime to work on personal projects that aren't necessarily in their job description. Workers can use the time to develop something new or to think about how to fix something that's broken. The idea is to allow workers time to feed their own curiosity and creativity.

The concept is controversial, though, and certainly not universally accepted. There are a lot of potential problems with it. For example, how can you ensure the worker is doing anything at all with his or her day to sit and think? What if workers are using company time and resources to scheme up a new product that they will patent on their own? And does time to go off and follow one's own interest work counter-intuitively to a workplace culture that is supposed to encourage teamwork, collaborative effort, and synergy among workers? And if the 20% concept works so many miracles in boosting creativity and innovation, why doesn't every company do it?

At best, the 20% concept does offer some scope for employees to dream up new, creative ideas, and clearly some companies like Google seem to think it's effective. And it does give a nod to the importance of creativity in the workplace. But at worst, it's a simple waste of time that cannot be monitored or measured, and discourages teamwork. It's really up to individual companies to gauge if such a program is right for their workforce.

Do the Opposite

One way to jolt your brain out of its regular patterns of thinking can be to purposely expose it to different stimuli. For example, the next time you're at a magazine rack and you notice yourself gravitating toward the same magazines that you always pick up and read, select a magazine that you have never read before. It doesn't matter what it is. Buy the magazine and spend at least 15 minutes flipping through it. Read an article. Look at the pictures. Notice how it is different from your favourite magazines. Try to picture the kind of person who would normally buy this magazine. You're likely to pick up a magazine about, say, fly fishing, and complain that you have no interest in fly fishing and want to put it back. But that is precisely why you *should* buy that magazine. It is a discipline to expose your mind to unfamiliar—even unpleasant—stimuli. The jolt to the brain may be just enough to give you an idea, or a potential solution to a problem with which you've been struggling at work.

Get Your Crayons Back

Fortunately, boosting creativity in the workplace does not have to cost the company money, nor does it need to involve taking the entire staff out of the office for an offsite team building day (although these can be extremely useful if done properly). But here's where Canadian workers may need to take some personal responsibility for their own individual level of creativity.

Writer, cartoonist and blogger Hugh MacLeod is the author of a book entitled *Ignore Everybody: and 39 Other Keys to Creativity*. On his website he writes:

> Everyone is born creative; everyone is given a box of crayons in kindergarten. Then when you hit puberty they take the crayons away and replace them with books on algebra, etc. Being suddenly hit years later with the creative bug is just a wee voice telling you, "I'd like my crayons back, please."[50]

This could mean, quite literally, getting your crayons back. Drawing, doodling, sketching and other ways of stimulating the visual parts of the brain can be an excellent way of kick-starting creativity. This works even if the problem that needs solving is not particularly visual. The main idea is to jolt the brain out of one way of thinking and get it going on something else.

Daydream Believer

In the summer of 2010, the *New York Times* ran an article titled "Discovering the Virtues of a Wandering Mind" by John Tierney.[51] In it, Tierney explores the usefulness of daydreaming and how, in fact, it could actually be vital to creativity:

> In the past, daydreaming was often considered a failure of mental discipline, or worse. Freud labeled it infantile and neurotic. Psychology textbooks warned it could lead to psychosis. Neuroscientists complained that the rogue bursts of activity on brain scans kept interfering with their studies of more important mental functions.
>
> But now that researchers have been analyzing those stray thoughts, they've found daydreaming to be remarkably common—and often quite useful. A wandering mind can protect you from immediate perils and keep you on course toward long-term goals. Sometimes daydreaming is counterproductive, but sometimes it fosters creativity and helps you solve problems. ...

"For creativity you need your mind to wander," (Dr. Jonathan Schooler of the University of California Santa Barbara) says, "but you also need to be able to notice that you're mind wandering and catch the idea when you have it. If Archimedes had come up with a solution in the bathtub but didn't notice he'd had the idea, what good would it have done him?"

Who would have thought that a little idle brain time wasn't such a waste of time after all? Dr. Schooler, quoted in the article, goes on to suggest that activities such as jogging, taking a walk, knitting or just sitting around doodling seem to free the mind to wander in productive ways.

Art, Creativity and the Economy

Many artists have attempted to calculate the amount of economic activity generated by their presence in order to justify public funding of the arts. They conclude that, because of the money artists spend and the taxes they pay, they are making a significant contribution to the economy. They use this argument to lobby for greater public support and speak of the great return on investment that governments would reap through their financial commitments to artists.

While the "economic contribution" argument is technically true, we don't think this is the strongest possible justification for the arts. If governments paid people to dig holes and fill them back up again, these workers would be spending money and paying taxes, too. And if return on investment to the economy is the only goal, studies have concluded that the very best bang for the tax buck comes from spending on construction and infrastructure.

Artists and arts organizations, on the other hand, are doing something much more valuable than digging and filling holes. They are providing opportunities for people to expand their minds, see the world in new ways and open channels of creativity that will ultimately result in a more productive workforce. They also help build great cities and vibrant communities that are attractive to the international talent Canadian businesses and universities are trying desperately to attract. These are the true contributions that the arts make to the economy—and in their justification for why the arts should be supported, arts groups should be emphasizing this rather than trying to calculate how much money artists pay in taxes.

As Figure 3 outlines, the benefits of a vibrant arts and culture sector are numerous and range from aesthetic value to incubating the creative minds that will drive an expanded knowledge economy.

FIGURE 3: Potential Benefits of a Vibrant Arts Sector

Intrinsic Benefits	beauty
	increased understanding of the human condition
	entertainment
	mental, emotional and spiritual stimulation
	inspiration
Community-Building	brings people together
	increases understanding of other cultures and perspectives
	highlights common heritage and shared experience
	enlivens public spaces
Direct Economic Value	economic activity (e.g., ticket sales, jobs)
Spin-Off/Indirect Economic Value	tourism
	construction (e.g., of a new gallery)
	spin-off industries (e.g., catering for film crews)
Gravitational Pull	attracts people (talented people, skilled people, wealthy people, creative people and keeps them in place
	attracts businesses who realize the importance of a vibrant arts and culture sector
Creative People 1.0 Better Labour Force	more productive
	more innovative
	better problem solvers
Creative People 2.0 Next Generation of Labour and Entrepreneurs	when kids have access and exposure to a range of arts and cultural outlets, they grow up to be not just more interesting and more fulfilled people, but better workers and problem solvers *in all sectors of the economy*
Creative People 3.0 Knowledge Economy	places that have lots of arts and cultural outlets are better equipped to take advantage of the benefits of the knowledge economy

Making art and creativity a vital part of Canada's economic DNA involves simultaneous action on three fronts.

1) A Solid Footing

The first front is to ensure that the arts in Canada are on a solid footing. Some may consider artists as economic vampires—a bit self-indulgent, sucking resources and wasting time rather than making any positive contribution. This attitude needs to replaced by the awareness of the role of the arts in cultivating an environment conducive to a creative and innovative economy. Canadians should consider the arts as valuable for what they do for their hearts and minds, as well as for what it does for the economy.

But putting the arts on a more solid financial footing requires support. Support for the arts may well come in the form of public funding, but it also has to come from individuals buying tickets, going to shows, bringing art into their homes, paying for their children to take fine arts at school and so on. As long as the arts are seen as a luxury or waste of time rather than as a key part of Canada's economic DNA, Canada will underperform in the global economy in the very area it has the most potential going forward: the knowledge economy.

2) Arts and Education

The second front is the education system. We want to be clear that educators are not on trial here. Generally, most teachers in Canada are doing a great job, and we recognize that creativity is not entirely absent in the current system. There is a reason why Canadian students are consistently near the top of the global rankings.

But for all that it is doing right, there is room for improvement. Canada's current education system is not particularly good at unleashing the creativity and entrepreneurialism inherent in students. If Canada is to become a giant in the 21st century international knowledge economy, it needs a revolution in education aimed at bringing out and fine-tuning the creative capacity of students from pre-school to grad school.

Not every young student will thrive in an arts immersion program, so the task is to design learning environments that work for a broad range of students but still include a larger dose of creativity cultivation. But whatever methods are used in education—be it arts immersion or a more traditional teaching model—fostering imagination and creativity will require that the arts play a critical role.

3) Arts and the Office

The third front in this battle is the workplace. CEOs, executives, managers, supervisors, human resource specialists, headhunters, shareholders and investors need to place a greater value on the arts and the creativity-generation potential it possesses. Those companies that "get this" will have a competitive edge. There will not be a standard template that businesses can follow as each will have to find its own way to bring creativity into the workplace, but the theme is one that applies across the economy.

Doing this goes beyond just placing some nice art work in the boardroom or making a donation to a local arts group (although these are welcomed). It's really about making an intentional effort to infuse creativity in everything the company does. Reward employees who show creativity. Hold team building exercises in museums or art galleries, rather than in bland meeting rooms. Creative workplaces and employees have to sprout up across Canada's economic sectors, from mining and farming to video-game design and health care. If this does not happen, the Canadian economy will not be able to compete at a top level in the global knowledge economy.

With success on all three of these fronts will come a shift to a more creative Canadian society, one that will be the foundation from which Canadians can vault themselves higher up the value chain and capture jobs in the knowledge economy. In this future, businesses look for and nurture creative employees; investors look beyond quarterly income statements and accept the risk of backing truly innovative approaches and ideas; schools and universities foster creative students; and individual Canadians seek out and support the arts to a much greater degree than they do now.

The Fountain of Creativity

The word creativity runs the danger of being overused in current discussions of economic development. The same holds true for the word innovation. It would be a shame, though, if they end up in the heap of tired business school clichés because they are extremely useful and important economic assets.

Creativity is the process of having original ideas that have value. And as we have seen, the value attached to any creative idea can often go beyond a market price. But the processes of invention, innovation and design describe how creative ideas add *economic* (i.e., commercial) value. All three are unique processes in how a product is developed. All three potentially add value to our lives and the economy. And the generation of all three requires one simple thing: *a creative mind*.

Education is a key player when it comes to fostering a creative society. Learning through the arts is one of many ways educators have found to engage children in the learning experience. The product is children who *learn how to learn*. And at their core, they are creative. But creativity must not be limited to children. Canadian adults are potentially creative, too, even if they don't believe they are. The arts, often underappreciated in our society, play an important role here. As well, employers have a responsibility to play by fostering a workplace that is creative.

There is also personal responsibility in the creative process as well. Like anything worth possessing, a creative mind demands action on the part of the individual. If you are struggling with a mental block at work, or needing to find some creative inspiration, take matters into your own hands.

The Canadian economy needs more creativity. Coming up with new processes, inventions, innovations and designs is critical for keeping up in the rapidly changing 21st century global economy. It's up to each one of us individually to change our attitudes and intentionally choose to embrace creativity.

Successful movement on the three fronts of creativity in Canada's communities—financial support for the arts, arts in education, and arts in the business world—will go a long way in changing Canada's economic DNA, allowing it to compete with the best of the best in the global economy. The result will be (ideally) a Fountain of Creativity from which Canadian businesses can drink. The innovation that this yields will enable Canada to capture large pieces of the global knowledge economy pie and to hone its competitive edge in natural resources and high-end manufacturing as well.

The next chapter discusses another imperative for the Canadian economy, but one that relates in many ways to creativity: developing a more cosmopolitan attitude.

Chapter 7

More Than Tourists – Developing a More Cosmopolitan Economy

"I am not an Athenian or a Greek, but a citizen of the world."
— Socrates

"The whole world is coming after talent."
— Professor Arvind Gupta, CEO and Scientific Director of MITACS Inc.

In the last chapter, we discussed the economic importance of becoming more creative and innovative. Another way to broaden our minds and increase our scope of thinking is to embrace the habit of looking far and wide for inspiration, customers and business partners. In short, Canadians need to become more "cosmopolitan."

We use the word cosmopolitan in this chapter to refer to the bundle of traits, attitudes and behaviours that connect us to the global community. A cosmopolitan society or business sector is one that is culturally diverse, welcoming to foreigners and foreign ideas, active in the global community and market, confident about what it has to offer the world and enmeshed in international partnerships of all kinds. A cosmopolitan spirit will drive a more competitive Canadian economy—one that flourishes in the global marketplace.

Cosmopolitanism is the itch that makes you want to see what's going on one town over. It's the drive to trade with strangers from across the sea and find business partners in other countries. It's the new perspectives and creative ideas that come from connecting with people from different cultures. It's the trust that comes from friendships that span borders. It's the thirst to compete with the world's best rather than hunker down and play it safe at home. Cosmopolitanism is what enables people and businesses to take advantage of the opportunities that exist in the wider world. It's the means by which we can harness the forces of globalization and make them work to our advantage.

The future of Canada's economy lies in the ideas Canadians generate and, in turn, transform into profitable commercial ventures. This will not happen to the degree needed to sustain Canada's economy over the long-term in domestic isolation. It requires meaningful and durable connections with people in other countries that go far beyond the fragile buyer-seller relationship. Indeed, the more international Canadians are—and the stronger their ties with international partners—the more likely it will be that Canadian ideas will turn into profitable ventures—now and in the decades to come.

Cosmopolitanism, it should be stressed, is not a lack of attachment to Canada. Cosmopolitanism is most virulent when it arises out of a deep and abiding connection to Canada. If Canadians are to be successful out in the wider world, they need to have something of value to share and to keep them from losing their way. That something is the love they feel for Canada and the conviction that what they have to offer the world is valuable.

A cosmopolitan spirit will lead some to try their luck elsewhere. It will also draw people to Canada. This ebb and flow of residents is part of the bargain. Canadians have to be willing to see some of their best and brightest leave Canada. At the same time, they have to create an environment at home that will entice expats to return and cause talented potential immigrants to seek out Canada. Canadians cannot rest on their laurels. If Canada wants to be a magnet for talent, it has to earn it anew each day.

Cosmopolitanism will help give Canadians the edge they need to succeed in the global arena. Those who play it safe and stay home will not only miss out on the action, they will find that the safety of home will not protect them from a falling standard of living. It's the array of perspectives and choices that defines a cosmopolitan society, not their assimilation into a bland cultural soup.

Cosmopolitanism must also go far beyond mere tourism. Vacationing abroad is fine, but it's really the tip of the cosmopolitan iceberg. Canadians must do more than pass through other places; they need to sell to, work with, learn from and truly know their foreign friends, customers and competitors. They must participate in the wider world, not just ride a tour bus through it.

A Change of Attitude

To become a truly cosmopolitan society, Canadians will have to change some attitudes and accept at least two things that go against their natural inclinations.

First, battening down the hatches and embracing trade protectionism is an economic dead end. Free trade is not a perfect system, but like democracy, it's the best we've got. Canadian businesses that can't compete in an open global market will fail eventually no matter how many tax dollars or protectionist regulations are thrown at them. Like it or not, Canadians live in the age of globalization. What's more, the last thing Canadian businesses need is for other countries to throw up walls that keep Canadian businesses out. Protectionism hurts everyone.

As such, well-intentioned but ultimately misguided "Buy Canadian" movements and supply management in agriculture (especially dairy) only turn up the temperature on our little frog in the pot. Hiding from our competitors is not as smart as rising to the challenge they present because you can't hide forever. Canada's strategy should be to out-perform foreign competitors, even if this means that some Canadian suppliers fail. An open global economy requires Canadians to not only compete at the highest level, but also to accept that foreign suppliers will be better at some things. This means being ready and willing to adjust and to let go of industries at which others are superior. The alternative option is to become like Albania—isolated, cutoff from global opportunities and dirt poor as a result.

Second, adopting a cosmopolitan approach means that Canadians need to get really comfortable with change and uncertainty. Canadians will have to be familiar with a wide range of cultural practices and be willing to try new things. They will need to adopt what Salman Rushdie calls the "migrant perspective." Because migrants live in different cultures, they have a richer understanding of the strengths and weaknesses of both their original culture and their new one. They are, as a result, able to embrace the best of what they see and jettison the worst. This is not an easy or comfortable process. Identity is called into question and paralysis can develop in the face of too much change at once. In addition, not all cosmopolitan experiences will be fun or even positive, but they can all be learning experiences.

The potential paralysis can be avoided if Canadians play the economic game with a strong sense of what it means to be a Canadian (and why this is good) and maintain deep roots in their local communities. It is one thing to be open to other ways of thinking and doing, but quite another to let this overwhelm or undermine what Canadians have to offer *as Canadians*. As noted, cosmopolitanism is about appreciating multiple perspectives and being comfortable in international settings; it is not about losing your sense of self as an individual or as a country or adopting cultural relativism. Nonetheless, the migrant perspective will challenge many heartfelt beliefs and inject a large dollop of discomfort into formerly comfortable situations. Canadians will need to suck it up and enjoy the game rather than go home with their tail between their legs; taking your toys and going home leads to, at best, mediocrity and, at worst, economic collapse.

Fortunately, and as with other themes discussed in this book, Canadians are not starting from scratch. Canada is already one of the most cosmopolitan countries in the world. It has a diverse population, immigrants seek it out, it is a trading nation and it attracts large numbers of foreign students, vacationers and investors.

But there is no doubt that Canadians can do better across a broad range of fronts from attracting more foreign students and accrediting the skills immigrants bring with them to being more aggressive in international business and integrating global experiences into the education system.

Seeing Things Differently

Creativity flows out of cosmopolitanism. Gregory Berns is a neuroscientist who has applied his research to the study of economics and how the brain comes up with new ideas. In *Iconoclast,* Berns outlines patterns of thinking and habits of people who are just that—iconoclastic. These are the thought leaders, the innovators, the ones who dare to take steps not thought possible. And ultimately, it is the iconoclasts in our society who have the ability to take the world to places not thought possible. Think of people like Thomas Edison, Henry Ford, Walt Disney, Florence Nightingale, Martin Luther King, Pablo Picasso and Steve Jobs. Not all of us are (or should be) iconoclasts. But studying their minds does yield some insight into how so-called regular people can become more creative.

One of the primary traits of the iconoclasts is that they literally see the world differently than everyone else around them. Sometimes this happens strictly through chance, as in the case of extreme geniuses like Einstein. Other times, though, the ability to see things differently can be induced. Berns identifies the way a normal brain functions by placing things it sees and observes into "categories." We observe the world around us and automatically categorize things in certain ways depending on our past experiences. This can limit our idea-generating abilities, especially if our categories are too narrow. Fortunately, we can take steps to change that. Berns explains:

> Sometimes a simple change of environment is enough to jog the perceptual system out of familiar categories. This may be one reason why restaurants figure so prominently as sites of perceptual breakthroughs. A more drastic change of environment—travelling to another country, for example—is even more effective. When confronted with places never seen before, the brain must create new categories. It is in this process that the brain jumbles around old ideas with images to create new syntheses.[52]

In other words, we have the ability to intentionally "shock" our brains out of established patterns of thinking by introducing new stimuli.

Where Did You Do Your OE?

One very practical way to engender this is to encourage and facilitate Canadians to live and work abroad for an extended period of time. This need not apply solely to young adults, but the years immediately after high school or university are the most opportune time for an experience of this sort. The responsibilities of later life (e.g., children, mortgages) often make extended stays overseas difficult for people in their 30s and 40s.

There are precedents for this. In Australia and New Zealand, for example, an OE (overseas experience) is part of the culture. And in the UK, the "gap year" is the common expression referring to the year between school and work in which living elsewhere is part of the learning experience.

Young adults may also go abroad as tourists or as students, but these would be seen as separate experiences from an OE. The difference lies in the degree of immersion in the foreign culture—the more immersed in the local culture Canada's young expats are, the better. Staying for at least a year and actually working rather than backpacking or attending classes provides for a particularly enriching experience. There is nothing wrong with being tourists and students—both should be encouraged—but the goal is to go beyond what these options offer and really get to know life and work in another country.

Some of those who go abroad won't come back. But many will. And they'll come back with new ideas, increased confidence, foreign contacts and a better sense of the global economy and how to connect with it. This will not automatically translate into productive economic activity back in Canada. After all, working as a bartender in Buenos Aries, an intern in Washington DC, or a bank teller in Paris is not going to magically turn young Canadians into international business wunderkinds. What it will do, however, is create a culture in which thinking beyond Canada's borders is the norm.

Imagine a new employee working for an architectural firm in Toronto that spent two years doing construction and other odd jobs in Europe. Let's call this young man Evan. Evan's OE in Europe (made financially possible by working while there) allowed him to spend a lot of time observing European architecture. His construction jobs illustrated some of the differences between the construction sites he worked on at home in Ontario and how the Europeans do things. He even got to know the daughter of the owner of a large construction services firm based in Berlin. These experiences made Evan the ideal choice to tag along with the senior architects to discuss a partnership with a German company to design buildings for a major Chinese development project. It is these sorts of synchronicities that, over time, will give Canadian firms an important edge in the global competition for wealth.

The Buy-In

For the OE to become commonplace in Canada, buy-in from parents is critical. Of course, there are plenty of parents in Canada who have encouraged or will encourage their children to go live and work abroad for a year or two, even if the job they find (e.g., bartender, nanny, fruit picker) may not appear to be in line with their chosen field of study. Many of these parents may have experienced their own year abroad as young people and immediately recognize the benefits of it.

But unfortunately, it is not yet the norm in Canada for parents to nudge their children in this direction. Many parents, in fact, would actively discourage (even prohibit) the idea, downplaying it as impractical and a waste of time. Some would discourage it out of fear—fear of their child choosing to stay abroad or even fear of the possibly that their child will encounter negative influences or even physical danger. These are legitimate fears, but ones that need to be overcome. The benefits of living abroad far outweigh the risks.

Support and buy-in from parents is important, but not sufficient on its own. Employers in Canada need to start recognizing the benefits of workers who have lived abroad, rather than scanning a resume and looking at time spent out of the country as an indulgent holiday. For example, if employers see the value of hiring people with an OE under their belt—and reward rather than penalize this experience—it would go a long way in instilling the OE as a common practice in Canada. Application forms could be designed to include space for applicants to specify international experience (outside Canada and the US) of 60 days or more; CVs could include an "international experience" category after education and before employment history.

Similarly, schools could develop programs highlighting the benefits of an OE and how to plan one. And just as the need for driver training has caused numerous driver education businesses to spring up, the needs of young adults doing their OE will be serviced by businesses that assist with everything from choosing a destination and potential employer to language training and travel insurance.

The practice of living and working abroad needs to become a social norm such that peer pressure, the expectations of employers, the encouragement and financial support of parents, the advice of educators and the cues of pop culture work together to make the OE a natural and appealing part of the transition to adulthood. Working overseas for a couple years should be like learning to drive—something that is expected of, and desired by, young adults.

Obviously, having done an OE is not a sufficient reason to hire someone and it is not a substitute for completing post-secondary education. The OE is just one piece of the human capital puzzle.

Welcoming the World

If encouraging Canadian young people to live and work abroad for a year or two is a benefit, then surely the flipside of the coin is valuable too: encouraging foreign young people to come to Canada to do their OEs. If Canada can attract lots of young people from other countries to live and work in Canada, some will stay to make up for the Canadians who don't come back. Others will go home with all sorts of personal connections to Canada that will expand its international presence.

This will take some work, however. As we argue in Chapters 4 and 5, Canada tends to fly under the radar for a lot of the world. Canadians know that they have fantastic cities, a vibrant culture, incredible natural places, stable political systems and a strong economy—but not enough of the rest of the world is aware of this. The problem with being so low profile, then, is that Canada may not be the top-of-mind choice for young people from around the world when they are considering places in which to do their OE. Canadians need to change this by telling Canada's story more enthusiastically. And if young Canadians start traveling and living abroad in greater numbers, they will be Canada's most influential ambassadors.

Another way to attract talented and energetic young people from abroad involves transforming the post-secondary system into the "go-to" place for the world's students to come and get educated. To paraphrase the disembodied voice in the movie *Field of Dreams,* "…if you build a great education system, they will come." This includes not only universities, but also polytechnics and trade schools which are likely to play an increasingly important role in training and providing vital skills for the global economy.

Unfortunately, too many of us either never think about foreign students or think that they are somehow taking scarce spots and funding away from Canadian students. The reality is that foreign students typically pay high rates of tuition and, in this way, help fund the lower rates paid by Canadian students. Foreign students are a money-making proposition for Canada's post-secondary schools. For this reason alone, the more the merrier!

In addition to the revenue boost, international students bring their "foreignness" with them. By their very presence, students from abroad make Canada's post-secondary schools more cosmopolitan. In theory, this rubs off on both the faculty and the Canadian students with the result being substantially more interesting school environments, a broadening of perspectives on the part of both the foreign and domestic students and friendships (not to mention romances) that span international borders. If you want Canadians to have a broader outlook and an affinity for global business, mashing them together with international students is a great place to start. The most obvious sites to do this are universities and colleges where foreign students are around for several years and thus have time to develop real relationships.

Opportunities for foreign exchanges also exist at the high school level and through organizations such as churches and youth groups. For those familiar with the sitcom *That 70s Show*, Canada needs a "FES" (foreign exchange student) in every class in its schools.

When the foreign students return home, they bring with them an appreciation of the great country that is Canada and they leave behind revenue to sustain and improve Canada's schools. Canadian students learn about other cultures by hanging around with the foreign students and, in some cases, economic ties may be created as young entrepreneurs develop individual relationships or even networks that have the potential to blossom into international partnerships and enterprises.

Of course, none of this happens if the foreign students have their heads buried in their books (or laptops) the whole time they are in Canada or if they only socialize with other foreign students. Steps need to be taken to ensure that voluntary apartheid does not take root on campuses. It would be a huge missed opportunity if there is a lack of actual interaction among the foreign and domestic students. Interaction can be facilitated by proactive efforts to promote socializing, working, learning and living together.

Attracting Entrepreneurs

It's not only foreign students looking to do a year or two overseas that we should be targeting, but also skilled entrepreneurs and "connectors" who are looking for a place to set up shop. Canada has always been a top destination for many international migrants, but too often they are limited to asylum seekers or those fleeing persecution in other lands. Refugee policies aside, Canada has done a less-than-stellar job at attracting bright, energetic entrepreneurs—some of which have enough capital to start up a great business idea in Canada, but not the time or patience to go through the immigration process. Others don't have the required $300,000 in personal cash to qualify as potential immigrants under the federal entrepreneurship program.

A *Globe and Mail* editorial addressed this problem:

> Canada has both human capital and financial capital. But it is not so good at finding connectors who can bring new ideas and existing cash together to create businesses and jobs. That is a special group, and application forms alone won't bring such entrepreneurs to the fore—it takes their presence in Canada, and then, a demonstrated ability to convince investors. ...one idea worth considering is the Startup Visa, in which entrepreneurs (often recent university graduates) could get a work permit if they have a given amount of venture capital backing. ... In economic terms, we often think of immigration as a way to fill jobs and put existing skills to good use in Canada. Let's not forget that entrepreneurship and innovation, in and of themselves, are skills we need more of.[53]

A Vancouver-based group called Startup Visa Canada seeks to do exactly this. The group is advocating for changes to Canada's immigration system that would make it easier for would-be entrepreneurs to come to Canada and set up shop:

> Currently, the federal and provincial governments' entrepreneurial immigration programs contain minimum personal fixed asset provisions of about $300,000 and a long approval process that make it nearly impossible for today's immigrant entrepreneurs to start companies here.

> The Startup Visa Canada Initiative would create an additional new visa program that:

> → would allow for an investment of $150,000 into a newly formed Canadian technology startup to qualify in place of the minimum asset provisions.

> → would enable approved local investor(s) to endorse qualified entrepreneurial immigrants to obtain their temporary work permits. This permit would only allow the immigrant to work for a newly formed company, and thus not take jobs away from qualified Canadians.

> → would require immigrants to have at least a one-third equity position in their companies, be active in management and create at least 3 full-time equivalent (FTE) jobs over the course of a 2-year program period.

It would be truly fantastic if Canada could beat the US to the punch and be the first to extend an invitation to the best entrepreneurs out there: Entrepreneurs of the world, Canada is open for business![54]

Eric Brooke is a spokesman for Startup Visa Canada. "The intent should be to create new jobs," Mr. Brooke said. "The concern is to ensure we have the skills we need in Canada to create the new companies that are going to wow us."[55]

Other nations are waking up to the advantages of attracting the global entrepreneur class and Canada could fall behind. Recent changes in the UK have seen the investment requirement from entrepreneur applicants fall from £200,000 to £50,000. And in the United States, the Startup Visa Act is being put before the Senate (largely through the efforts of former presidential candidate John Kerry). The ideas are being supported by New York Mayor Michael Bloomberg. "We will not remain a global superpower if we continue to close our doors to people who want to come here to work hard, start businesses and pursue the American dream," Mr. Bloomberg said. "Today we may have turned away the next Albert Einstein or Sergey Brin.[56]

Attracting Academics

Attracting international faculty to Canadian schools is another major stimulant of cosmopolitanism, both on campus and off. In a paper about how to transform Alberta's universities into the best schools in the world, former University of British Columbia President Martha Piper suggests hiring large numbers of Nobel Laureates.[57] This is the type of change that will be necessary if Canadians are to have the best, most cosmopolitan schools in the world.

Of course, none of this will be easy to achieve. Canada needs to provide fantastic educational programs and research facilities so that international students and professors will be drawn here (this will also be of great value to Canadian students). This means investing heavily in Canadian schools and working hard to attract the best minds to them. Fortunately, English is a language that many foreign students know or want to learn (Canada also has French programs for the world's Francophone population). Still, more effort to ease the transition to studying in Canada would be needed as would the efforts to ensure actual interaction between local students and between foreign students and Canadian society more generally.

As with other elements discussed in this book, half measures will not get the job done. Adding a few extra spaces for international students, for example, is not sufficient. What is needed is change on a transformative level. Canada's universities need to become known as hotbeds of international learning. Bright students from around the world need to be dreaming of attending the University of Alberta or McGill University rather than just Harvard or the London School of Economics. Canada's campuses need to be overflowing with foreign accents. When the political science club holds a model UN, it should be able to have actual people from each country participating.

Is Canada Up to the Task?

It's fine to say that Canadians should be working harder to attract foreign students, entrepreneurs and academic researchers. But if they come, can Canadians make room for them?

This comes back to the comments made by Arvind Gupta, CEO and Scientific Director of MITACS Inc. that were noted in Chapter 5. Gupta suggests that Canadian schools are not in the sights of the best students in India. According to him, India's top students with the highest grade point averages head to Stanford or Princeton, or to Australia, Britain, France and Germany where schools have been more aggressive in targeting students from India. "These kids are not knocking on (Canada's) door," says Prof. Gupta. "The whole world is coming after talent."[58]

Will this focus on foreign students and entrepreneurs push Canadian kids out of the way? There is no reason why it should. Indeed, the ideal is to have Canadian students and entrepreneurs mixing with international newcomers and watching the exciting, dynamic ideas that come out of it. To ensure this, Canada's universities and polytechnics will have to grow to make room for the additional foreign students. Hefty tuition rates for foreign students will help pay for this (and the scholarships that would allow bright put poor international students to come to Canada), but Canadians may well have to pump more money into their post-secondary schools. Being the best—the best faculty, the best labs, the best libraries, the best students—will not come cheap. There is a reason a Ferrari costs more than a Ford.

If encouraged to come to Canada to study, some of these bright foreign students will end up staying and, in turn, will add badly needed skills to the labour force. If this is not the best way to attract skilled immigrants who will flourish in Canada, we don't know what is.

But is this a form of pillaging young talent from countries desperately in need of educated people to help solve local challenges? At least in some cases, it certainly is. We don't feel too sorry for parents in, say, England forking out a small fortune to send their kids to schools in Saskatchewan or Nova Scotia. And if some of those students decide to stay in Canada, well, that's the game called the international economy. Why shouldn't smart, talented people who want to come to Canada get the chance?

Things get a little grayer when you imagine a young person from an impoverished country being lured away by a school in Canada to swell its ranks of skilled and creative workers. On the other hand, if the opportunities are not available in a person's homeland, shouldn't they have the chance to study in Canada and, if they wish, stay and seize those opportunities?

As global citizens, Canadians will have to find ways to strike a balance between being competitive and being caring and decide when attracting the world's best talent becomes poaching the human resources of other nations. This moral challenge, however, should not deter Canada from offering the world its educational services, nor should Canada close its doors to bright, international entrepreneurs and academics who see attractive opportunities in Canada.

Reading Cosmo at Work

Cosmopolitanism must also be facilitated by employers. As mentioned, employers need to see the value of international experiences such as OEs (even if they do not directly relate to the job at hand) and they need to find ways to harness the cosmopolitanism of employees. It is not enough to check off an "international exposure" box during an interview and then do nothing to integrate the cosmopolitan assets employees bring to the workplace.

In addition to cultivating and utilizing cosmopolitan human capital, Canadian businesses need to take a cosmopolitan approach to their operations in general. This means that they need to look to the wider world for everything from suppliers and customers to ideas and inspiration.

Take a small printing company that pumps out fliers and small print runs like annual reports for local companies: what would it gain from being more cosmopolitan? It may be able to learn from how print shops in other countries operate; it may see the early signs of changes to the domestic printing market by observing trends in foreign markets; it may find a cheaper source of supplies; it may benefit from staff who have worked abroad who have brought back innovative ideas; it may even find an international partner who would like to work on projects over the Internet. The list goes on and on. This does not mean that the print shop owner should spend all day researching printing in foreign countries or networking at international printing industry conventions. The point is that a business culture that is cosmopolitan presents Canadian businesses—even if they are not overtly international—with a wide range of possible competitive edges.

A strong cosmopolitan streak is particularly important in businesses that either are, or could be, active in the global economy. Canada's population of 34 million is only a fraction of the global population and, in turn, only a fraction of the global market, investment pool and talent pool. Canadians sitting on their duffs and ignoring the opportunities presented by the global economy is like a store only being open for an hour every second Wednesday.

Moreover, many Canadian businesses only make sense if there are international customers buying what they have to sell. Canadians don't need all the oil, food, timber, auto parts and maple syrup that they produce. And speaking frankly, Canadians need the wider world more than it needs them. Hence, Canada can't afford to be anything but cosmopolitan.

In her book *Why Mexicans Don't Drink Molson*, Andrea Mandel-Campbell makes no bones about it—she thinks that Canadian businesses are wimps when it comes to the international economy.[59] Canadians drink Corona but Mexicans don't drink Molson because Canadians are too timid when it comes to selling their products abroad and working with international partners. To put it another way, Canadian businesses are not cosmopolitan enough. There are exceptions, but the general picture Mandel-Campbell paints is one of international mediocrity and wasted potential.

Largely Irrelevant?

In a July 2011 commentary, well-known Canadian business commentator and journalist Eric Reguly bemoaned the enormous list of companies which at one point were Canada's ambassadors on the international business stage—companies like Inco, Falconbridge, Dofasco, Stelco, Algoma Steel, MacMillan-Bloedel, Molson, Alcan, Ipsco, Gulf Canada, Newbridge Networks, Poco Petroleum and Masonite.[60] All of these one-time Canadian giants have been snapped up by international competitors, diminishing Canada's role and profile in the business world.

Why doesn't Canada have more international corporate champions? According to Reguly:

> There's no paucity of excuses from Canada's political right, middle or left for our poor global showing. Corporate tax rates are too high? They're among the lowest in the Western world. There's too much government coddling? There's too little. Canada is too small? The Swiss wouldn't buy that argument. Costs are too high, and training and education are inadequate? CEOs can't endure Canada's winters? Celine Dion intolerance? Blah, blah, blah.[61]

The reason, according to Reguly, is none of these. He blames Canadian investor greed and short-sightedness. Every time an international buyer comes knocking with an offer, shareholders of these former Canadian giants started salivating and took the offer. Reguly believes that Canadian investors would have been better off refusing some of the "take-the-cash-and-run" offers and, instead, becoming the buyers rather than the sellers.

Reguly isn't alone in his observation—even Canada's foreign competition recognizes it. In his commentary, Reguly quotes Don Argus from comments made in 2008 when he was Chairman of BHP Billiton, the British and Australian-owned largest mining company in the world. "Canada's policies are a worst-case scenario," said Argus. "Canada has already been reduced to an industry branch office and is largely irrelevant on the global mining stage."

Canada has to stop becoming "largely irrelevant" in the international arena. Canadians not only need to welcome foreign investment when it is to their advantage, but they also need to be bolder and longer-term in their thinking about investment abroad. Canadian businesses do fairly well in terms of investing outside the country, but they should also think bigger in terms of acquiring larger corporate giants. As Reguly suggests, this will take some longer-term vision.

Go Forth and Multiply

This chapter has argued that Canadians must build on their already strong international connections and make the country a truly cosmopolitan place. In corporate boardrooms, on factory floors, around drafting tables and in front of computer screens, people from all corners of the world and in all sorts of languages need to be asking: "Do we have the Canadians involved in this because they know their stuff." The economy is a global system and successful jurisdictions are those that not only compete with other jurisdictions, but also those that team up with them to generate new ideas to create wealth.

Canadians need to see the rest of the world as more than just a market and more than just a threat (although it is both of these things). This requires getting out there and building international business relationships with individuals, firms and governments—not to simply sell wares, but to collaborate on new ventures as well. Canadians have done a great job shipping oil, beef and auto parts to the US, but it's time to make some significant additions to the nation's economic repertoire. Canada can, and should, become a global trendsetter in international business.

Encouraging more students and young people to live and work abroad for a year or two—the overseas experience (OE)—could become a central part of this strategy. Up until now, Canadian culture has not tended to expect or even recommend living abroad as an essential part of gaining life skills and broadening perspectives, but it should. This will require an intentional shift in thinking and attitudes on the part of parents, employers and individuals.

On the flipside, attracting more foreign students, entrepreneurs and academics to Canada would also inject a more cosmopolitan perspective into the economy. Canada is already one of the most open countries in the world and immigration has added to its population and labour force. Immigration also comes with some challenges of its own, but the benefits of a growing skilled workforce outweigh the costs. This is particularly true if Canada can be turned into a destination of choice for the best and brightest people in the world. Canada's global competitors are already a few steps ahead of it in this regard—Canada has some catching up to do.

And of course, in the corporate world, Canada needs to up its game. Short-sightedness has limited Canada's presence in the global business world. In order to prevent becoming "largely irrelevant," Canadians need to start thinking more about the longer term.

Cynics will say this is wildly naïve—Canada is a small player and it will never be a trendsetter or leader in international business. This sort of self-defeating nonsense needs to be ignored. There is absolutely no reason why Canadians cannot be partnering with Indian firms to develop biotechnology, or with Russian gas explorers to provide innovative gas field services, or with the Chinese to design more sustainable cities. Nor is there a reason why Canada's universities and polytechnics cannot market themselves more aggressively and compete with the best schools in the US, the UK and Australia.

None of this will happen spontaneously, though. Building international business relationships in places like India and China takes time, effort and energy. And making some intentional changes to the way Canadians think about living abroad will take some getting used to.

Canadians are every bit as capable of becoming cosmopolitan as any of their global neighbours. Canada is overflowing with highly educated, entrepreneurial people with a great deal to offer the global economy—it just has to take more advantage of these assets. Canada has the wealth, multicultural society, political stability and the freedom to experiment and create. The Indigo chain of bookstores has always promoted Canadian authors, proudly proclaiming: "The World Needs More Canada." How true! But Canada needs more of the world as well. Becoming a truly cosmopolitan society requires more of each.

Chapter 8

Moving Up the Value Chain

"The path of least resistance is what makes rivers run crooked."
— Elbert Hubbard

"Gerry Price is a proud Canadian, the head of a company that has been making ventilation equipment for commercial buildings in Winnipeg since 1946. Strip out the emotion, though, and Mr. Price can't think of a good reason to build anything in Canada."
— *Globe and Mail*

In the old days when people were sent to poorhouses for falling on hard times, there was a job called "picking oakum." Workers in this hapless industry untwisted old bits of hemp rope by hand until their fingers bled. The resulting product was then used for other purposes such as stuffing mattresses. As such, picking oakum was a "value-added" industry: a raw material was processed and, in turn, value was added and jobs were created. It's easy to imagine a local oakum producer stressing about how much better it is to untwist the hemp locally as opposed to exporting it in its raw form.

Picking oakum is an extreme example, but it highlights the need for economic strategies that go beyond simply promoting more value-added activity. A new meat packing plant, bitumen upgrader or auto parts factory are fine, but alone they are not sufficient to maintain Canada's economic prosperity in the global economy of today let alone 2025 or 2050. Canadians have to aim higher—much higher—than the modern equivalents of picking oakum.

This does not mean that Canadians shouldn't make pasta, furniture and other value-added manufactured products when and where it makes economic sense to do so. What it does mean is that Canadians need to fully understand that simply "making things" (especially things that their competitors can make cheaper) will not keep Canada prosperous.

For example, Canada has lots of oil and natural gas liquids that could be turned into plastic patio chairs. But the reality is that, even after shipping the chairs across the sea to North America, the Chinese can still make plastic patio chairs cheaper than Canadians can (assuming wages and environmental standards are not lowered—something Canadians definitely do not want to do). As a result, when some guy in Florida needs a patio chair, he buys the one made in China. And at $9.99 each, you have to sell a lot of patio chairs to fuel your economy.

So where does this leave Canada? Believe it or not, it puts it in a very enviable spot. The Chinese officials who know that their country's long-term economic future will be bleak if it relies on making stuff that ends up in dollar stores would love to have the advantages that Canada has right now: a modern service-based economy with a high level of education, a relatively low level of poverty and infrastructure galore. Indeed, one of the reasons that the Chinese economy is growing is that it is building the things Canada already has. Canadians have everything they need to aim for the top of the global value chain.

The industries in which Canada has a chance to develop a comparative advantage are largely at the upper end of the value chain. You don't want an army of workers assembling DVD players. What you want are workers who design the next generation of DVD players (which will probably not even be DVD players) and other marketable innovations. You want businesses that not only figure out how to extract oil and gas in Canada, but that sell their expertise to drilling ventures around the world. Canadians might make lots of pasta out of their wheat or they might ship it elsewhere for processing, but what they really want is to corner the market for designing the strains of wheat and other staples that will help feed the world's growing population.

And best of all, jobs at the high-end of the value chain are better paying and generally more interesting and fulfilling.

Canada has all the right ingredients—wealth, education, previous successes, entrepreneurs, great cities and so on—to play at the high-end of the value chain, Canadians just need to make this their focus. *Exporting natural resources and "making stuff" will remain important components of the Canadian economy.* But if Canadians don't aggressively go after the profits and jobs to be found in medical research, education services, financial services, engineering, marketing, biotech, IT, entertainment, etc., they will find their standard of living falling as their competitors get better and better at both the bottom and top ends of the value chain.

Sarah Kutulakos, Executive Director of the Canada China Business Council, sums up the challenges Canadians are facing and the attitudinal change that is required. "[Canadian companies] need to understand that rather than making or selling a widget, their role may be in the widget's technology, or the processes that underlie the design of the widget. Adding value often requires thinking about your company's skills more in a three-dimensional way, rather than just a straight two-dimensional, traditional way."[62]

This chapter discusses what it means to truly be a "value-added" economy. We profile some of the examples—both from Canada and abroad—of adding value, and why in fact losing some manufacturing jobs may actually be a benefit for Canada. The chapter concludes with a challenge to Canadians and Canadian companies to aim higher when it comes to value-added opportunities.

Stop the Outsourcing? What for?

There has been a lot of angst over the past decade or more about the "outsourcing" of manufacturing jobs. While the uproar has been greater in the United States, Canada has not been immune. There have been more than a few examples of Canadian manufacturing companies moving some of their work abroad to take advantage of cheaper labour.

But is outsourcing really all that bad? It depends on what jobs are being outsourced and which ones are being kept at home. The example of the Apple iPod provides an excellent lesson. Researchers at the Personal Computing Industry Center at the University of California, Irvine, have broken down the "value-added" components of an iPod retailing at $US 299. Figure 4 shows the breakdown.

At the time of the study, the iPod was being assembled in China by a Taiwanese company. This may have had some Americans up in arms when they realized that iPods—a symbol of American genius and enterprise—are not made in the good ol' USA.

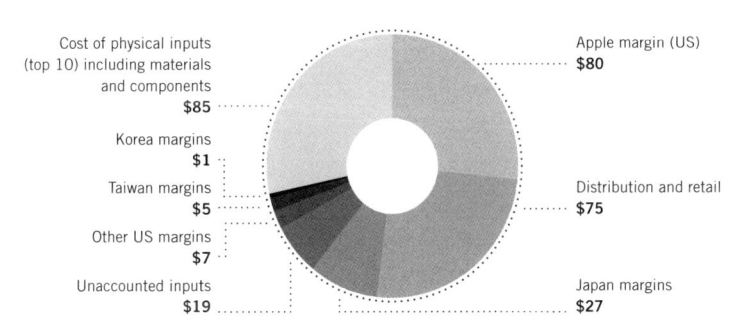

FIGURE 4: Breakdown of iPod at $299 Retail Price

Cost of physical inputs (top 10) including materials and components
$85

Korea margins
$1

Taiwan margins
$5

Other US margins
$7

Unaccounted inputs
$19

Apple margin (US)
$80

Distribution and retail
$75

Japan margins
$27

Source: Greg Linden, Jason Dedrick and Ken Kraemer. 2009. "Innovation and Job Creation in a Global Economy: The Case of Apple's iPod." Industry Studies Association 2009 Annual Conference.

But according to the research, only about 2% ($5) of the cost of the $299 iPod accrues to those workers in China who snap the tiny contraption together. Another 9.5% ($27) accrues to Japan, the home country of Toshiba and Matsushita, high-tech companies that developed the hard drive and display modules of the device. By far the largest share of the value-added stays in America, with $80 of each iPod flowing directly into the coffers of Apple's head office in Cupertino, California. Another $75 goes to the retailing and distribution, much (but not all) of which would be in the US as well.

The upshot of the research is that only 2% of the value-added in the production and sale of an iPod flows to the country where what we traditionally think of as manufacturing—the assembly lines of people and machines snapping the iPod together—actually takes place.

> While the iPod is manufactured offshore and has a global roster of suppliers, the greatest benefits from this innovation go to Apple, an American company, with predominantly American employees and stockholders who reap the benefits. ... Apple keeps its product design, software development, product management, marketing and other high value functions in the US. This is not necessarily because the US workforce has superior capabilities in all of these areas, but because Apple has developed very specialized knowledge and ways of doing things that reside within the company and would be difficult to transfer to external locations.[63]

Design. Develop. Market. Manage. These are the high-skilled jobs that Americans (and Canadians) are able to provide which add far more value to the product—and the profits of Apple—than do the assembly lines in China.

The study by the University of California researchers goes on to estimate the number of jobs attached to the production of the iPod and the earnings of those jobs. The data reveal even more insight into the value-added game. In 2006, it is estimated that iPod related jobs (including production, retail, engineering and other professional) in the US totalled 13,920. Non-US jobs were more than double that at 27,250. However, iPod workers in the US earned an estimated $753 million, while workers outside the US earned $318 million. While China accounted for the largest number of jobs outside the US, Japan earns by far the largest share of the non-US wages ($102 million) because of the higher value-added in the small hard drives and video displays.[64]

"The relationship between innovation by US companies and employment in the US is more complex than phrases such as the 'vanishing middle class' suggest. When innovative products are designed and marketed by US companies, they can create valuable jobs for American workers even if the products are manufactured offshore," argue the UC Irvine researchers. "So it appears that innovation by a US company can benefit both the company and US workers, even if production is offshore and foreign suppliers provide most of the inputs," conclude the three researchers.

There is, however, an important caveat to this discussion. While innovative North American companies may be keeping the higher-paying "brain" jobs at home, there are still thousands of workers in North America who are not in this high-skill work category. They are the stranded ones whose jobs are at risk (or already long gone). What about them? It's fine to point out that the engineers, marketers and legal advisors of companies like Apple are doing just fine, but what about the low-skill domestic workers? Does their plight count for nothing?

The cleavage between high- and low-skill domestic workers and their expected economic outcomes poses an enormous problem for political leaders who are expected to "do something" to stop the exodus of manufacturing jobs. Even if it they are low-paying, some of the 11,715 jobs in China assembling iPods would be welcome relief, especially for laid-off workers in the US industrial heartland where unemployment coming out of the recession remains painfully high. In April 2011, the unemployment rate in Michigan—one of the hardest hit manufacturing states—is 10.2%. In California, the home of Apple Computers, the unemployment rate is 11.9%.[65] While Canada's manufacturing heartland has not been hit as dramatically in terms of unemployment, the same anger about outsourcing jobs overseas would be felt if a Canadian company was laying off people in Ontario, for example, and shifting jobs to China.

This is all the more reason to shoot higher in terms of skills and education. The impetus is on North Americans to ensure they are as smart as possible, a point that the UC Irvine researchers make in their conclusions: "It is more important than ever that all children receive an education that prepares them for 21st-century jobs. Retail jobs are no substitute for higher paying services employment. ... Unfortunately, the continuing loss of manufacturing jobs, which pay better than retail jobs, means fewer opportunities for non-college educated workers. Even the administrative jobs that pay reasonably well at companies such as Apple often require a higher level of education."

The Israeli Example

In the book *Start-Up Nation* by Dan Senor and Saul Singer, the nation of Israel is held up as an excellent example of a country in which innovation, creativity and the willingness to risk failure are part of the culture. The result is a small economy that has flourished with new start-up companies, particularly in high-tech sectors, moving it way up the value chain.

"How is it that Israel—a country of 7.1 million, only sixty years old, surrounded by enemies, in a constant state of war since its founding, with no natural resources—produces more start-up companies than large, peaceful, and stable nations like Japan, China, India, Korea, Canada and the United Kingdom?" ask the authors. The secret to Israel's success, according to Senor and Singer, is built into the DNA of the country. The DNA the authors talk about is not the genetic kind. It is the attitudes and perspectives on life and the world with which Israelis are raised.

Part of the explanation is the fact that, even before its inception as a physical country, Israel was under attack by its neighbours. And certainly after it was established in 1948, it has been surrounded by neighbours who would like to see it eliminated. That kind of adversity and unfriendliness has made the world outside of the Middle East an attractive place for many young Israelis, and travelling abroad as part of one's life experiences is almost as important as formal education itself. Most Israelis are well-traveled and cosmopolitan, a trait which has yielded valuable perspectives and creative ideas that are brought home and incorporated into start-up business ventures.

As well, Israel is one of only a few developed countries that requires its young people to serve a minimum of two years in the military. The military organization, however, is not at all like that typified by the top-heavy, authoritarian style of military in the US and most other countries. Because of a series of events and evolutions over the years (which are well documented by Senor and Singer), Israel's military style is very open and collaborative. Lower ranking soldiers and personnel are almost expected to challenge authority. What would be viewed as completely unacceptable insubordination in the Canadian, American or most other armies is viewed as constructive participation in Israel's. It is what the authors describe as *chutzpah*.

Apparently, *chutzpah* is carried from the compulsory army into colleges and universities. Students are freely encouraged to challenge dogmatic thinking, including whatever may come out of the mouths of professors and instructors. In North America, this comes across as brazen and combative—impolite! But for Israelis, it is an attitude which has given rise to some of the most creative and innovative small business models around.

Two other countries in the world have grown up in similar circumstances to Israel: South Korea and Singapore. All three have compulsory military requirements, all three have lived next to inhospitable neighbours and all three place a strong emphasis on post-secondary education (especially in engineering and science). Yet compared to Israel, South Korea and

Singapore are laggards when it comes to innovation and the establishment of start-up high tech companies. What's the element that Israel has that the other two are missing? Senor and Singer explain that in both South Korea and Singapore, an overly enthusiastic devotion to order, rules, and authority have crushed what is sometimes called "fluidity"— the ability to shake things up a bit and have creative ideas fall out.

"Fluidity...is produced when people can cross boundaries, turn societal norms upside down, and agitate in a free-market economy, all to catalyze radical ideas. ...Thus, the most formidable obstacle to fluidity is order. A bit of mayhem is not only healthy but critical," say Senor and Singer. The authors also point out that, in South Korea's case, the unwillingness to admit failure is another enormous stumbling block in that country's ability to kick-start innovation. Saving face may be highly valued socially, but it kills entrepreneurialism.

The list of Israel's strengths—its culture of challenging authority, its worldly cosmopolitanism, its fluidity—has without question helped vault it into becoming the "economic miracle" that it is today. Can these traits be easily transferred to other countries? The implication of the book *Start-up Nation* is that other countries can learn from Israel and adopt some of its good habits. But is it that easy? How much of it is really unique to Israel and its (quite often) unhappy story? Is Canada at a disadvantage because it is *not* surrounded by hostile neighbours? (If so, there really isn't a practical solution since provoking the US into hostility is unlikely to be a successful economic development strategy for Canada.)

As for *chutzpah,* can it be learned by a new generation of Canadians? Should Canadians encourage young people to be less willing to accept authority and rules? Do Canadians really want to do this? In fact, Canadians don't have to become Israelis soldiers with *chutzpah.* Nor do they have to dump their natural qualities like politeness, consensus-building and appreciation for order. But, they may have to temper these default characteristics if they are getting in the way of creativity, innovation, and moving up the value chain in the global economy.

Not a Bad Situation for Canada?

Mike Moffatt is a lecturer in the Business, Economics and Public Policy (BEPP) group at the Richard Ivey School of Business and the co-owner and co-founder of Nexreg Compliance Inc. In an interview with the *Globe and Mail* in June 2011, Moffatt had some pointed words about the future of manufacturing jobs in Canada:

I'm afraid there won't be [a place for unskilled workers in the new economy]. Or at least not that many. [Canada's] advantages are going to be in higher-quality, higher-tech parts, that are difficult for low-cost jurisdictions to replicate. That's not a bad thing. Most of the value-add comes from the design and manufacture of higher-end components, so this is not a bad situation for Canada to be in. It doesn't create as many jobs, but the jobs it does create are much higher value or pay.[66]

While it may seem tempting to suggest that Canada's manufacturing will be completely hollowed out by low-cost competitors, this is not the case. However, it will take some brilliant thinking and shrewd business planning for Canadian companies to find a high value-added niche in the mix. Continuous innovation by Canadian manufacturers in product design, automatic processes, marketing, services and new business models will be key.

Jayson Myers of Canadian Manufacturers and Exporters is positive about the future of manufacturing for this very reason. "I am optimistic about Canadian manufacturing because of the value-adding opportunities that will be available within our own domestic market. But, instead of looking at how we can simply upgrade resource processing, businesses need to focus on how they can leverage their capabilities to provide solutions in the form of high value products, technologies, and services," says Myers. "There's an opportunity to leapfrog into world-class leadership capabilities in extraction and processing technologies, resource and environmental management, logistics and trade facilitation. But again, all this depends on changing business habits and business models."[67]

The importance of this will only heighten in the future as Canada's competitors are themselves getting increasingly into the design and engineering game. At the same time, countries with low-cost labour such as China are increasingly eyeing the higher paying jobs and farming out the low-skill assembly jobs to other countries just as Canada and the US have done.

That's the way ya do it!

There are, of course, plenty of examples of Canadian companies using their brain power to pull themselves up the value chain. And not all of these are in what we typically think of as "knowledge" industries like software development or biotech. Some of the best examples are in the heart of traditional manufacturing.

Consider the unique and innovative approach taken by MW Canada, a Cambridge, Ontario manufacturer of textiles used in window shades. By all accounts, MW Canada should have gone the way of the dinosaur years ago, succumbing to a similar fate as dozens of other textile manufacturers in Ontario over the past few decades. After all, can't the Chinese and other low cost labour countries do it all cheaper?

Well, China may be able to do it cheaper, but not if they haven't thought of it yet. MW Canada is kicking it up a notch by experimenting with nanotechnology, much of it developed in Canada. Instead of just reflecting all of that nasty sunlight and keeping it out of houses (the role of traditional window blinds), MW Canada is making use of the sunlight. The next-generation blinds being developed by MW Canada will collect solar power and use it to recharge items inside the house such as phones, laptops and iPods.

Innovation, learning, discovery, pushing boundaries—it's apparently in the DNA of the company. "We have a full-time research and development person on site who does research into new materials and is a liaison with universities," says Robert Berger, who runs MW Canada. "Staying ahead of the technology curve is the only way to survive against low cost competitors in Asia."

The learning doesn't stop with the one full-time research person, either. MW encourages continual staff education and training. The company has been recognized as a leader, winning national and local awards for workforce training and development. The company has an education room with a bank of computers that employees use to upgrade their education and skills.

Employees at MW Canada go through a skills assessment and get individualized programs that can be done over the web. They do everything from upgrading literacy and getting their high school equivalency papers to post-secondary degrees. Some companies would scoff at the cost of providing this kind of skills development, but not Robert Berger. "It is part of our cost of doing business, because it is part of our future," he says.

The recession hit MW Canada as badly as it hit everyone else—maybe even worse. The company depends on the US for 70% of its sales of window blinds, and the downturn in the American housing market south of the border was certainly felt. From the middle of 2008 to the spring of 2009, sales slumped significantly. MW Canada had to lay off employees and reduce work weeks to three days. "But we told our employees the education room was open and this was the time, more than ever, to accelerate their skills," Berger says. Now, as business gradually picks up in the post-recession period, the company will be much better positioned than most.

It is precisely this kind of creative, innovative business mindset that Canadian manufacturers need to develop. The company did not turn inward and "stick with its knitting" by making the same old product that had served it well for so many years. Nor did it fold up shop claiming that taxes and labour costs made for an unfair playing field in Canada. They took what they knew (window blinds), added a new twist to it (nanotechnology), invested in their staff (education and skills development) and are coming out on top.

Or consider the story of E.H. Price Ltd., a Winnipeg-based manufacturer of ventilation systems and equipment for commercial buildings. They've been proudly Canadian-based since 1946—yet they have moved almost all of their actual manufacturing to places where it is less costly such as Arizona and Georgia.

Sounds like another hollowing-out of Canadian manufacturing story, doesn't it? Except that what E.H. Price has done is use Winnipeg as its base of the higher-end operations, essentially the reversal of what Canada has been used to: foreign companies doing research and development in their home country while setting up branch plant operations in Canada to assemble it. That model is outdated, and E.H. Price is showing how Canadian-headquartered companies have the chance to take advantage of a high-priced loonie and highly-educated workers while sending the lower-paying, lower-skill jobs elsewhere.

"The company has moved production of high-volume, 'commodity' products to the United States. Winnipeg, in turn, is the hub for research and development, patenting and software development, as well as production of key niche, custom and low-volume products. It has 60 workers dedicated to R&D. The company's success rests on a significant investment in innovation—developing new products, tools and manufacturing processes for its plants in both countries. 'If we didn't develop new products, Winnipeg would be gone for us,'" says Gerry Price, head of the company, in a *Globe and Mail* interview.[68]

If Canadians are smart, the examples set by MW Canada and E.H. Price will pave the way for a whole new kind of mentality around value-added manufacturing in Canada: keeping head office functions at home along with the engineering, branding, research and development, and perhaps some of the very specialized, niche fabrication. But that will take some intentional changes in mentality.

The Second Mouse

It has often been said that the early bird gets the worm. But sometimes, especially when it comes to the economy, it is the second mouse that gets the cheese! This lesson can be seen when it comes to companies looking for their position on the value chain. It should be reassuring to know that being creative and innovative doesn't mean you have to come up with a totally original idea; rather, the trick may be to take an existing idea, tweak it, and find a unique way to capitalize on it.

Malcolm Gladwell observes that there is a difference between innovation and originality and that it is sometimes the late-comer to the party who makes it big in commerce. Speaking at the Cannes Lions International Advertising Festival in June 2011, Gladwell expands on an article he had written for *The New Yorker*.[69] The story focuses on Apple co-founder Steve Jobs, who in late 1979, paid a visit to a Xerox innovation laboratory. There he discovered two of the tech giant's big ground-breaking innovations: the computer mouse and the graphic user interface. Xerox never followed through on these innovations, but Jobs smelled a winner. Returning to Apple, he and his team of engineers refined the technologies and eventually cashed in enormously on them. Both the mouse and the graphic user interface are often associated with Apple, but both were actually lifted from an original innovator.

"If you look at the history of Apple, they're always the last to the party," said Gladwell. "They've made a business out of being late." Steve Jobs, he added, "is the archetypal entrepreneur of our age, right? And he is not an innovator, right? He's the guy who comes second or third and makes it better."[70]

Canada has often been thought of as a branch-plant economy dominated by huge multinational corporations where much of the research and development work is done in the home country and parachuted into the Canadian branch plant once it has been perfected. In a sense, this model of production may make some sense: why do all the heavy lifting and spending on R&D if someone else is going to do it anyway? Isn't this the "second mouse" approach identified by Gladwell and others?

But this misses the point of adding value. Being an innovator—even if it is "borrowing" an idea from elsewhere and tweaking it—is not the same thing as simply implementing a process or a design that the foreign-owned multinational has developed. The branch plant model adds no value; it simply executes orders. True value-added in manufacturing, natural resources or high tech involves either commercializing new research or implementing existing research in a new and profitable way.

Movin' On Up

Moving up the value chain is one of the most important moves a Canadian firm can make. In the 21st century, it's no longer preferable, it's critical. And while traditional notions of adding value are fine, Canadians need to rethink what truly adding value means in a very rapidly changing global economy where the competition for every imaginable job is heating up.

A lumber company turning logs into lumber is value-added. An oil sands company turning bitumen into refined gasoline is value-added. A food producer turning agricultural commodities into chicken nuggets is value-added. And all made important contributions to the Canadian economy in the 20th century. But for Canadian firms in the 21st century, true value-added will require aiming much higher than this.

In the forestry sector, for example, a Canadian value-added company may be the one to research and develop new techniques for harvesting trees and be able to export that knowledge around the world. Another company will be a globally recognized leader in building and engineering lumber mills, finding the most energy efficient and waste minimizing techniques. Still another company will be a leader in understanding sustainable forestry management techniques and market the know-how in other countries. A company will not just cut and export lumber, but will design totally new kinds of structural building products that don't even exist yet.

In the energy sector, a value-added company will be the one that not only refines crude oil, but also refines new techniques for oil extraction. Another company will add value in the energy sector by designing new systems for carbon capture and sequestration, a technique which has yet to be proven effective or cost efficient, and teach the world how to do it. Yet another energy company will push the boundaries on clean energy such as solar, geothermal, and tidal, making Canada a global go-to place for the engineering and design of renewable energy systems.

In agriculture, value-added will go far beyond the animal slaughter house. A value-added company will be developing new strains of crops that are more resistant to drought or flood. Another will design new irrigation techniques that not only increase crop yield, but reduce waste of valuable water resources. Still another will export meat while developing alternative non-meat food sources to growing populations in the developing world.

And in manufacturing, value-added will mean not just passively assembling items for a foreign company, but rather activity pursuing the higher-end functions that require creativity and imagination. Not just assembling 20th century cars, but dreaming up totally new transportation systems for a crowded 21st century world. Not just making up batches of pharmaceuticals developed elsewhere, but building on existing research to create and patent new drug treatments in Canada. Not just churning out widgets that are shipped to assembly lines elsewhere, but innovating and exporting brand new production processes—even ones that may make the widget obsolete.

Jock Finlayson, the Executive VP and Chief Policy Officer of the Business Council of British Columbia, gets it:

Canada is well known as a resource producing nation—a powerhouse in energy, metals and potash, and a significant global presence in forest products and parts of agri-food. As such, Canada should also strengthen its capacity as a supplier of services and technologies that increase the efficiency of resource use and minimize the environmental consequences of this kind of industrial activity. To sustain our position as a globally competitive resource producer, Canada needs to be a centre for excellence in areas like waste management, carbon capture, energy efficiency, and the development and deployment of smart electricity grids.[71]

One of the first reactions that some readers may have at this point is what we believe to be a bad habit: blame government and turn to it for solutions. Too few tax credits for R&D, too much regulation and red tape, too little emphasis on helping firms export—the list of complaints goes on and on. We are the very first to admit that getting the public policy and tax framework correct is very important. But we also believe it's wrong-headed to blame everything on the government. It's a bit like a bratty teenager who doesn't want to practice the guitar protesting that his guitar is not of high enough quality. "If this guitar wasn't such a piece of junk, I could play a lot better." There is some truth to this—a high quality guitar would probably be easier to play and may sound better. But it's also a cop-out to blame his inability to play on the guitar alone. Practice and attitude are more important than an expensive guitar.

All of these value-added propositions require Canadians and Canadian businesses to intentionally decide to aim higher than where they've traditionally aimed before. And without question, thousands of Canadian firms are doing exactly this. Our point is not that Canadians don't know how to do it, but rather that Canadians in general may still be aiming too low.

It doesn't come without effort, but to be truly a value-added economy, Canada can't waste any more time underachieving. From the individual worker and sole proprietor all the way up to the boardrooms of the biggest corporations in Canada, we need to collectively decide: *let's aim as high as we can.*

Chapter 9

Embracing Risk & Accepting Failure

"Every project should be a little bit impossible.
That is how we progress."
— Brazilian architect Ruy Ohtake

"Never tell me the odds."
— Han Solo, The Empire Strikes Back

Most of us are familiar with a little blue and yellow can of spray in our garages or under the kitchen sink called WD-40. That is the trademarked name of a lubricating spray developed in 1953 by a Californian named Norm Larsen. It was originally designed to repel water and prevent corrosion, and later was found to have a variety of practical household uses. WD-40 stands for "Water Displacement – 40th Attempt."

Fortieth attempt? You can almost hear Mrs. Larsen yelling down into the workshop: "Norm, sweetie, forget it! You've tried over 30 formulas...it's not gonna work!"

As investors and taxpayers, we are more likely to identify with Norm's wife than Norm. If success is not ensured, we get antsy. We want our mutual funds to go up and never down. We want ventures supported by government dollars to be a sure thing. This is not, however, how you succeed and make money in the long-term in a highly competitive and ever changing global economy.

Has risk aversion in Canadian society gone too far? Have Canadians become so intolerant of mistakes and errors that they go to enormous lengths to either hide them or pass them off as success in disguise? Some would say, quite emphatically, no! The fact that Canadians are perhaps more conservative and less risk-taking than others (notably Americans) is the single most important reason that Canada's economy weathered the global economic downturn of 2008-09 better than most. Canadians were not overleveraged up to their eyeballs. Canada's banks and financial institutions took a much more cautious approach to lending. As a result, the Canadian economy came out of the recession more quickly and in better shape than most. While banks around the world were tanking in 2008, not one Canadian bank or financial institution was in serious trouble and not 10 cents of public money had to go to prop up a failing bank. What's not to like about Canada's conservative attitudes when it comes to money and banking?

While it is true that a conservative lending approach did save Canada's hide in 2008, there is a difference between prudence and paralysis. In this chapter we explore some of these differences and suggest that what Canadians need is not recklessness, but boldness. And what prevents that boldness in most cases is simply fear.

Are Canadians Really Risk Averse?

Most of us may have a suspicion or general hunch that Canadians, by nature, are more conservative and less likely to take risks, especially compared with their neighbours to the south. But is this perception more myth than reality? Where is the hard evidence that Canadians are shy when it comes to making risky business decisions?

According to a survey commissioned by Deloitte Canada,[72] Canadian business executives do not *perceive* themselves as any more risk averse than Americans. In a national survey of 450 Canadian and 452 American executives drawn from small, medium, and large companies, Canadian business leaders' responses were distributed almost identically to those of their US counterparts. In other words, when asked about their own risk profile, Canadian executives viewed themselves as *no more or no less* willing to take on intelligent risk. These findings were very similar to another 2003 study by the Institute for Competitiveness and Prosperity.[73]

Deloitte's study took the analysis one step further. It contrasted "individuals' risk tolerances with the level of risk tolerance implied by the *actual decisions that they reported making* and the decision-making heuristics used to inform those decisions" (emphasis added).[74] The result of this analysis? Canadian business executives are not as tolerant of risk as they think they are. In the resulting index calculated from survey responses, American executives were, on average, 13% more tolerant of risk than their Canadian counterparts.

Lower risk tolerance in Canada is identified as one of the key problem areas for the Canadian economy by the Deloitte report. "Over time, firms able to undertake risk intelligently will generate higher returns and better productivity than their more risk-averse competitors."[75] But as we will discuss shortly, there is an enormous difference between running headlong into crazy business schemes, and (as the quotation from the Deloitte report suggests) taking on *intelligent risk*.

(And with all due respect to Han Solo of *The Empire Strikes Back,* quoted at the beginning of this chapter, we *do* think one should know the odds—we just don't think that they should drive one to complete inaction. But we appreciate Han's moxie.)

Dropping the Ball

In the book *Why Mexicans Don't Drink Molson*, Canadian journalist and author Andrea Mandel-Campbell makes a compelling case that risk adversity in the boardroom has been a big problem for Canada's international business profile. In terms of exports, foreign direct investment overseas, or marketing a "Canadian brand," Mandel-Campbell argues that Canada is falling dangerously far behind the rest of the global economy.

She identifies several factors that could lie at the root of this almost irrational shyness about doing business abroad: close ties to the US have never required Canadians to be active traders, Canada's former colonial status and a host of badly designed and counterproductive government policies and actions over the past century or so. Lots of examples are given of the golden opportunities Canadian firms have had to make a big forays into the international business world—but sadly, most of these chances were squandered.

The most spectacular example of Canadian businesses dropping the ball could be that of how Canada lost two mining companies in the span of twelve months. In the fall of 2005, Canadian mining giant Inco announced a proposal to acquire another big Canadian mining company, Falconbridge, for $12 billion. Much of the incentive for the merger was for each company to avoid takeovers by aggressive foreign firms. It would have created a truly giant, global player in the mining world—a Canadian "super major." But it wasn't to be. The two companies ended up as targets for hostile takeover bids from rival firms. Swiss-based Xstrata, already 19.9% owner of Falconbridge, bid for a complete acquisition, while Vancouver-based Teck Cominco sought to acquire Inco.

Later, in June 2006, US-based copper giant Phelps Dodge made a bid for the proposed combined Inco/Falconbridge company. The Phelps Dodge Inco Corp. would have been the fifth largest mining company in the world. Its corporate and copper division would have been headquartered in Phoenix and its nickel division in Toronto. But that wasn't the end of it. Swiss Xstrata upped its offer to acquire Falconbridge, a counter-offer that was nearly 10% higher than Inco's bid. Xstrata won it and absorbed Falconbridge. This left Inco without a dance partner, and soon became the target of Phelps Dodge and Brazil's Companhia Vale do Rio Doce (CVRD), which won out over Vancouver's Teck Cominco (now known as Teck Resources).

Two of Canada's mining giants squandered a chance to form a truly Canadian mining giant and, instead, were gobbled up by the Swiss, Americans and Brazilians. As Peter Munk, Chairman of Barrick Gold, ranted in a media article about the incident, "This opportunity will never arise again in your generation and not in your children's generation to put together a group like that. That's when you've got to have the determination and the balls and the courage."[76] It seems that what was missing on the part of Canadian companies in this situation was exactly that: courage. Similar themes of corporate timidity and nervousness about bold forays into the global business world have repeated themselves in other sectors in Canada from banking, resources and even brewing.

Mandel-Campbell laments Canada's risk aversion and warns that it will fall behind in economic standing and prosperity if Canadians don't do something to up their game. Her conviction is that Canada is entirely capable of this:

> Given what Canadians have been able to achieve at home, in such a harsh and unforgiving climate, (trading and doing business) abroad is eminently doable. If we can build ice roads across hundreds of kilometers of barren, treeless tundra that are able to withstand the merciless pounding of thousands of transport trucks as they make their way from Yellowknife to the diamond mines just south of the Arctic Circle, then we can do anything. It's a matter of first wanting to, and then familiarizing ourselves with the new topography.[77]

When Fear Takes Control

An old, familiar quotation still reverberates powerfully decades later. "...the only thing we have to fear is fear itself—nameless, unreasoning, unjustified terror which paralyzes needed efforts to convert retreat into advance."[78] The quotation appears in Franklin Roosevelt's first Inaugural Address of 1933. FDR was addressing the economic fear that was paralyzing Americans during the Great Depression.

Fear is a complex emotion. Some of the most recent neuroscientific research suggests that fear is recorded by the brain as memories in two distinct ways: one is through the part of the brain called the neocortex; the other is through a small, almond-shaped piece of the brain called the amygdala.[79] Both are important and necessary, but at times this dual system can cause problems.

Suppose, like many of us, you are at some point traumatized by a horrific event, say an earthquake or a car accident. The neocortex records the basic events that happened during the event—normal details like the weather that day, the song that was playing on the radio, etc. But the amygdala records the events in a different sort of way. Details are left out, but the overriding panic and dread of the situation is emblazoned on the brain and associated with the surroundings (the weather, the song on the radio, etc.). The neocortex is rational enough to remember the event as something in the past, something that no longer poses a threat. But the amygdala is on constant recall, and gives the brain the instinctual message that danger could be present when the environment is similar to when the event occurred.

"The trouble with emotional memories is that they can be fiendishly difficult to eradicate. The brain seems to be wired to prevent the deliberate overriding of fear responses. Although extensive neural pathways link the amygdala to the neocortex, the paths running in the reverse direction are sparse. Our brains seem to have been designed to allow the fear system to take control in threatening situations while preventing the reign of our conscious, deliberate selves," says Steven Johnson in his book *Mind Wide Open*.[80] For the present discussion, it suffices to say that fear is natural, and fear can indeed be useful in helping us avoid situations history has taught us to be dangerous. But fear, through the overriding power of the amygdala, can also paralyze us into inaction.

In the business world, paralysis is not often referred to as fear. Business leaders tend to avoid the word fear lest they be thought cowards. Instead, they wrap their fears into something that sounds much more scientific and practical: "risk management." Most people would rather say "there's risk associated with launching this product" than "I'm *afraid* to launch this new product," but they come down to essentially the same thing.

Risk management and risk analysis are, of course, useful tools to help quantify the probability of success or failure of any given business endeavour. But rather than using risk management as a tool to help understand the environment in which decisions are being made, too many businesses hide behind risk management as a way of chickening out on risky ventures. They have let fear take control. This is not to say that businesses or individuals should ignore risk and run head-long into any idea that comes along. Businesses should understand the risk, but not hide behind it.

Fear in the business world has its roots in three distinct kinds of fear: the fear of failure, the fear of rejection, and (most paralyzing) the fear of losing money.

1) The Fear of Failure

Failure at anything is never pleasant. Just like our WD-40 inventor Norm Larson, there must be a certain degree of frustration that comes with failed attempts. Yet all of us know on some primal level that failure is common—indeed often necessary—on the road to success. It's an age-old saying full of truth and wisdom: if at first you don't succeed, try, try again.

Yet despite knowing this, most Canadians (and the businesses they work for) are rather intolerant of failure. Perhaps because of a hyper-competitive economic environment, there is so much pressure to succeed that failure along the way is not an option. But all this really does is stifle innovation, creativity, and ultimately, success. It encourages inaction, which is the essence of the boiling frog metaphor. The frog feels the water heating up, but the fear of failure ("What if I can't jump high enough and fall back down into the water?") keeps him from taking action.

The critic will jump in at this point and argue just the opposite: accepting failure is the problem with the Canadian economy. Canadians wallow in mediocrity. They lack the competitive spirit that drives people to succeed at any cost. Canadians don't punish failure harshly enough. Canada is a country that's satisfied with "personal best" rather than demanding nothing less than the gold. It's a dog-eat-dog global economy, and the weak will be eaten! A stronger intolerance of failure is what is needed. Failure is not an option.

The problem with this line of thinking is that it ignores a fundamental truth: some degree of failure is unavoidable. "It's not *failure* that's not an option, it's *perfection* that's not an option. Canadians have to find ways to approach mistakes differently,"[81] says Alina Tugend, a columnist with the *New York Times* and author of the book *Better by Mistake: The Unexpected Benefits of Being Wrong*. "When we think that mistakes and failure are something to be avoided and dreaded, we close in on ourselves. And when we see mistakes as something to blame other people for and be defensive and not something to learn from, we can't move forward," says Tougend, who in her book argues that mistakes are everywhere. It's only when people admit to them, identify them correctly, and learn from them that they can move on to improvement and success. If the truth that failure is in some sense unavoidable is accepted, it liberates businesses to take some chances, to innovate and to be creative (the things urged in Chapter 6).

Another author on the topic of failure adds: "I think it's fascinating that ideas such as 'learn from your mistakes' have become such clichés, and yet we find it so difficult. The lesson I draw is that failure is pretty much inevitable. We've got long lives, we try a lot of things, and the world is incredibly complicated—things go wrong all the time. And we are not taught the right way to respond to failure," says Tim Hartford, author of *Adapt: Why Success Always Starts with Failure*.[82] Fear of failure should not be devastating. Taking a chance on a hunch should not be punished with a zero-tolerance approach to failure. We can't sit and wallow in failure, but we can come to accept failure for what it is—a necessary but sometimes unpleasant stepping stone on the path to success.

2) The Fear of Rejection

As social creatures, humans have become hard-wired for acceptance by their peers. From a young age, people learn to dislike—indeed, hate—being laughed at or thought a fool. Some of the cruelest displays of human nature can be witnessed among a group of children activity rejecting another child. It's heartbreaking to watch.

There are a number of theories why children do this. Perhaps it's to strengthen the group or to build character in individuals enduring the rejection. But whatever the reason, people carry this fear of rejection right with them into adulthood. Most people don't want to be different from the group. They want to fit in and they want to be accepted. This has serious implications for Canadian businesses and their constant attempts to come up with new and creative ideas.

A famous experiment in the 1950s by Polish-American sociology professor Solomon Asch demonstrates how powerful is the natural fear of rejection and how social pressure can actually alter the perception of reality.[83] The experiment involved eight volunteers, but seven of the eight were actors who were in on the experiment. The eighth participant was the only actual subject in the room. The eight participants were shown cards with four lines on them and were asked to identify which of the lines was closest in length to the first line on the card. Each was asked to give their answer aloud to the rest of the room.

The test was remarkably easy and should have caused no problems for anyone with average visual perception skills. However, when the seven actors purposely picked the same wrong answer, the one actual subject was often persuaded by "groupthink" to overrule what they knew was the right answer and go with the consensus. The experiment was repeated with several groups of actors and one non-actor, and the results were shocking. In the absence of the group of actors giving wrong answers, 95% of the non-actors could get every answer right all of the time. But in the presence of the actors giving wrong answers, only a quarter of the non-actors could achieve this perfect score. Most subjects succumbed to the "groupthink" about a third of the time.

Even more shockingly, when interviewed later about the experiment, subjects often admitted to changing their answers to fit in with the group, suggesting that they thought there must be some problem with their own visual perception. And while the subjects often knew that they were purposely overruling their own perception some of the time, most underestimated the number of times they made this intentional overruling, meaning that they were often completely unaware that they were doing it.

The findings of this experiment tell us at least two things: people want to fit in with what the group thinks and that this compulsion is so powerful that it can actually alter perceptions of reality.

This too has significance for Canadians and the companies for which they work. It's a familiar setting for many of us: sitting around a table with a group of co-workers, asked to brain-storm for ideas about new projects or initiatives the company could launch. "We want your ideas!" the bosses tell us. But how many of us feel hesitant to raise our voice and suggest an idea, lest the group thinks it's a poor one? Or if the group is coalescing around a certain idea, how many of us are brave enough to challenge it? The fear of rejection grips us in these social situations, often to the point where we are reluctant to suggest any ideas at all.

Dr. Patrick Finn, an instructor in the Faculty of Arts at the University of Calgary, identifies what he believes to be one of the most challenging problems in Canadian society: critical thinking. At a recent TEDtalks event held in Calgary, Finn surprised the audience by suggesting that critical thinking in Canada's education system is actually *stifling* creativity. Normally, "critical thinking" refers to a willingness to challenge conventional wisdom, taking an argument and seeing its many complexities and nuances. Critical thinking, by this conventional definition, is supposed to help—not hinder—the economy. But Finn's refers to critical thinking as the bad habit of smacking down any new idea and immediately seeing the fault in it. He believes that Canada's education system has essentially trained Canadians to be "intellectual ninjas" instinctively blocking a punch or a kick. The immediate reaction is to throw up a block to a new idea coming your way because it doesn't conform to your preconceived notions of what will—or won't—work.

"What we in the past called critical thinking is part of an old operating system that is now defunct. Our current educational system is geared toward the production of intellectual ninjas who are trained to efficiently attack and destroy incoming arguments. What we need now is 'loving thinking,' a form of creative cognition that engages with a plurality of ideas allowing the best to rise to the top," says Finn. "Part of my thinking on this is also that we cannot simply attack every idea that comes in because we are faced with an ocean of information and we would be drowned in its ebbs and flows. Unilinear critical thought was fine in the 19th century when we all read a few dozen books in a lifetime. It no longer works."[84]

Not only is this type of hyper-critical approach to ideas short-circuiting the generation of new ideas, it can also create an environment of insecurity in opening one's mouth. The attack of an idea while sitting around a table with co-workers is precisely the kind of social rejection that many of us fear, especially if it comes from someone in a senior position. The end result is a loss of creative ideas.

Consider a hypothetical dialogue between a worker named Sarah and her hyper-critical manager Raj:

> **Sarah:** *"I have an idea for a new project that could earn our company additional revenue. We could target university students looking for summer work and set up a for-fee website that would help them make some job connections."*
>
> **Raj:** *"That's been done a thousand times and it doesn't work. Students have no money, and besides, they're not the target market we identified in our last vision statement."*

Raj may not be intending this, but the message Sarah may hear is:

> **Raj:** *"You're an idiot."*

What if the response was this instead?

> **Raj:** *"Hmmm, well I know that others have tried this before, but what if we tweaked it somehow? Maybe we could find out why the students didn't use it and fix that problem. Or maybe rather than target students, we target companies looking to hire students and make connections that way? There may be an idea here, but could you do a little more work in fleshing out the details?"*

In the first response, Raj has slammed the door shut on an idea, and even worse, made it much less likely that Sarah will open her mouth again at the next brainstorming session. In the second response, Raj was still honest about the idea having been tried in the past, but attepmted to find a way to build on the idea. Most importantly, Sarah would leave the meeting feeling like her idea was valued—even if it was still half-baked.

In the workplace, Canadians need to develop some better habits around interacting with their peers. They need to stop instinctively responding to ideas with a "BUT that won't work because…," and replace it with "AND maybe we could add to that…". This requires some intentional changes in behaviour.

Without question, not every idea thrown out in a boardroom is a good one. Some are weak, some are bad, and some are outright terrible. But some are actually quite good—or at least potentially good. The important thing is to receive each idea that is voiced with respect, and not the hyper-critical reaction to which many Canadians default. This does not mean that Canadians should pursue every idea that comes along, but they must help diminish the fear of rejection that tends to hang in the room. If they don't, all ideas—bad and good—will go unspoken.

The classic, positive way to criticize is the praise sandwich. This basically involves three statements: "Hey, it's a great idea. There are some problems with it. But it's a terrific start." This is a better way to criticize than the fictional Raj's shoot-it-down comments above, but it can end up obscuring the constructive criticism with too much praise. John Lasseter, the hyper-creative head of Pixar Studios who has since 2006 been at the helm of Disney Animation, has a solution. His team calls it "PLUSSING"—which is simply taking something that is good and making it better.[85] The concept of PLUSSING is originally attributed to the creative genius of Walt Disney, but is now a driving philosophy at Pixar and Disney Animation. Rather than simply cutting an idea down, or hiding the criticism in a praise sandwich, the goal is to add to the idea—to "plus" it—by responding with phrases such as "Hey, wouldn't it be better if..." or "Couldn't we add this or that to make it better...?" The concept is twofold: one is to build up rather than tear down ideas; the other is to help ease the fear of rejection that most everyone experiences when it comes time to voicing ideas.

3) The Fear of Losing Money

The third general fear that can inhibit risk-taking and crush innovation is the fear of losing money. This is perhaps the trickiest to address in the context of risk-taking because, after all, who wants to lose money? A bright young person may have a great idea and a lot of enthusiasm, but the fact is that a lot of small business ventures fail. This would probably mean losing money—money borrowed from parents, friends, or banks.

The fear of losing money may be heightened when it is a publicly traded company. Who wants to face an annual meeting of shareholders to announce "Good news! We failed this quarter and lost a lot of your money. But failure will make us better...". It's a bit rich to suggest that corporate managers should not fear losing money when the money is not theirs in the first place. For these corporate leaders, it may not be so much the fear of losing money, as it is the fear of losing their jobs.

Business schools have long been preaching the gospel of success at any cost. Some of the most popular business publications over the past few years have been cheerleaders of financial success and achievement, not failure. Think Stephen Covey's *The 7 Habits of Highly Effective People* and Tom Peter's *In Search of Excellence*.

The other two fears—fear of failure and fear of rejection—pale in comparison to the mother of all fears: losing money or your job. How can this be reconciled?

There is, in fact, a healthy fear of losing money that perhaps should not be lost in this discussion. As discussed at the beginning of this chapter, fear is a natural emotion that has developed with the evolution of human physiology. It places a role in protecting us from dangers. The amygdala kicks in and does its job, and sometimes it saves our lives. When we see a bear in the forest or an icy road ahead of us, fear kicks in (or should) and we take whatever actions are necessary (backing away, slowing down) to preserve ourselves. That's natural, and it's a good thing.

But our relationship with money and income is more nuanced than that with a bear or an icy road. Losing money will not result in death. Yet it is perhaps one of the fears that grips us most deeply, often with paralyzing force. Companies too afraid to risk a new venture or launch a new product, or individuals too afraid to invest their money in an entrepreneurial idea, will ultimately impede creativity, economic growth and prosperity.

There are some signs, however, suggesting that the pendulum has started to swing the other way.

The April 2011 issue of the *Harvard Business Review* is dedicated to the theme of failure, which on the surface seems a bit of a departure for the publication. It's full of articles about famous CEOs with spectacular stories of failure and what they learned from them. The articles have a general theme of embracing failure as a valuable way to learn from mistakes. However, one column in the magazine by Daniel Isenberg, a professor of management practice at Babson College, dumps some cold water on the failure love-fest and adds some valuable perspective. "Embracing failure to encourage entrepreneurship is misguided. Failure should not be celebrated," writes Isenberg. "Well-intentioned though they may be, these attempts to celebrate failure are misguided. Fear should not be confused with anxiety—and celebrating failure seems aimed at reducing anxiety."[86]

Isenberg draws attention to the difference between fear and anxiety, and herein lies an important message. "Anxiety, Freud is said to have explained, is when you irrationally react to a simple stick as if it were a dangerous snake. Fear is when you react to a dangerous snake as if it were, well, dangerous. Anxiety is dysfunctional, but fear can be good," he says. The message for those would-be entrepreneurs or corporate management executives who are experiencing some paralysis around risky decisions is to distinguish between fear and anxiety. And of course, this is where risk analysis and actually knowing the odds (sorry, Han Solo) can play a useful role in helping quantify how dangerous the decision really would be.

The fear of losing money, income or business prestige isn't a 21st century phenomenon; it's actually been around for quite awhile, and it's been recognized as a problem for economic progress. Quintessential American business pioneer Henry Ford said: "Thinking first of money instead of work brings on fear of failure and this fear blocks every avenue of business—it makes a man afraid of competition, of changing his methods, or of doing anything which might change his condition."[87] The key is to properly assess risk, distinguish between rational fear and irrational anxiety, and not allow the fear of losing money to inhibit taking at least some chances.

Rolling the Dice

Are Canadians really too risk averse? Studies suggest that they are. Risk management techniques were supposed to be tools to help Canadians understand risk, but they have morphed into security blankets preventing them from making smart business decisions. Fortunately, Canadian economic history has had its share of "mavericks"—individuals who went against the herd mentality, took risks and accomplished great things. They also failed a lot along the way. The now-famous Leduc No. 1 oil well, drilled in Alberta in 1947, followed a string of dry holes. Had the original prospectors given up in fear of finding yet another dry hole, they never would have struck it rich in Leduc, Canada's oil industry may not have gotten off the ground and the country's prosperity would be much less than it is today. (What if modern risk management techniques had been around in 1947?)

Unfortunately, ridiculously skittish stock markets that go up and down if someone sneezes unexpectedly and a culture that favours economic comfort over financial adventure have pushed many of Canada's mavericks to the sidelines. "Stick with what ya know" is the all-too-common mantra of Canadian businesses. As a result, both public and private investment in bold new ventures is in very short supply.

Canadians need a higher tolerance for risk because failure is an unpleasant, yet necessary, means by which they will succeed. This may be a hard principle to accept in a culture where you have to appear to never fail or, at least, be good at blaming someone else when things go wrong. But tolerating failure doesn't end with the failed attempt. The failure needs to be accompanied by learning: Why didn't that attempt work? What did I learn that I can apply to my next attempt?

Ultimately, Canada's economic progress will rely on risk-taking. An entrepreneur has an idea, a scientist has a hunch, a designer has a vision. To act on any of these notions, someone needs to stick their neck out and take the chance, failure or not. But if the consequences of failure seem overly dire, they will crush the incentive for the risk-taker to try anything less than a sure bet. And the economy will suffer.

The fear of failure, the fear of rejection, and the fear of losing money—all three can act in ways that inhibit economic growth, productivity and prosperity. All will paralyze creativity and innovation. Yet all can be overcome and managed with some intentional actions on the parts of Canadians. Understanding the inevitability of some failure, incorporating lessons learned, "plussing" ideas and distinguishing between fear and anxiety can help move Canadians in the right direction.

Chapter 10

Green is the New Black

" Turn off the light and shut the fridge door—you are wasting money."
— Your Dad

Just about everybody will tell you that they care about the environment—sometimes while sitting on the seat of an ATV that has just ripped up a riverbank. Notwithstanding the gap between what people say about the environment and what they actually do, most people don't want to see toxic sludge in rivers, wildlife going extinct or smog-filled air. On some level at least, people get it.

Unfortunately, this doesn't stop us from kicking the environment in the stomach on a regular basis. How to reconcile the desire for environmental stewardship with the ongoing economic manhandling of the planet is a critical question—one that has been the subject of endless debates over the past several decades. It is far beyond the scope of our expertise to determine the best options for stewarding the planet's natural capital. Rather, this chapter is concerned with the following question: *how can treading more lightly on the planet give the Canadian economy a competitive edge?*

We do not argue that Canadian businesses need to be greener for the sole sake of improving the environment. A cleaner, less damaged world is doubtless a valuable by-product and one that serves the larger goal of a healthy planet. Rather, our premise is that a greener Canadian economy is a more efficient, less wasteful economy, and businesses that become greener will have a better chance of remaining viable vis-à-vis their less green competitors. In the pot of boiling water our frog has finds itself in, every competitive advantage is worth pursuing.

Also, we are not proposing some radical new form of economic organization. For some, the very term "green economy" implies a wholesale abandonment of capitalism and open markets based on a renewed relationship with nature and a strong emphasis on social justice. According to this school of reasoning, the neoclassical economic theory that underpins the current Canadian and global economy is completely out of synch with the limitations of the earth's ecosystems. From the ecological perspective, the neoclassical economic system must be jettisoned in favour of a new eco-economy. As Paul Hawken argues in *The Ecology of Commerce:* "If every company on the planet were to adopt the best environmental practices of the 'leading' companies ... the world would still be moving toward sure degradation and collapse.... Rather than a management problem, we have a design problem, a flaw that runs through all business."[88]

Another example of the ecological perspective is provided by Earth Policy Institute President Lester Brown:

> An environmentally sustainable economy—an eco-economy—requires that the principles of ecology establish the framework for the formulation of economic policy and that economists and ecologists work together to fashion the new economy. ... We have created an economy that cannot sustain economic progress, an economy that cannot take us where we want to go. Just as Copernicus had to formulate a new astronomical worldview after several decades of celestial observations and mathematical calculations, we too must formulate a new economic worldview based on several decades of environmental observations and analyses. ... Converting our economy into an eco-economy is a monumental undertaking. There is no precedent for transforming an economy shaped largely by market forces into one shaped by the principles of ecology.[89]

We, however, join others in taking a different position—one that rejects the idea that in order to save the planet we must smash to pieces the market economy that has served us rather well (with some bumps and bruises along the way, to be sure). We situate the green economy firmly within the current market-based global economy, or what we refer to as the *market perspective on the green economy*. An example of the market perspective is provided by the US Department of Commerce: support for a green economy "means encouraging the development of green products and services that contribute to economic growth and improve this nation's environmental stewardship. The jobs that are created and supported in businesses that produce green products and services, are green jobs."[90]

We argue that a *competitive edge* can be gained by becoming greener without abandoning capitalism, free markets, or the profit motive. Whether this will be enough to achieve the environmental outcomes needed to keep the planet healthy is left for others to debate. We are, however, confident that animating the green economic gene will improve Canada's economic performance as well as its ability to maintain its natural capital. Indeed, the efficiency and profits promised by more rigorous environmental standards demonstrate that "green" and "business" cannot only live together, but thrive together.

Other Definitions of the "Green" Economy

In a report funded by the Government of British Columbia, the Globe Foundation defines the green economy as "a fast-growing economic development model that focuses on the creation of green jobs, the promotion of real, sustainable economic growth, and the prevention of environmental pollution, global warming, resource depletion, and ecological degradation. Integral to the green economy are those elements of traditional economic sectors that are in transition to lower-carbon energy production and increased energy conservation in order to reduce greenhouse gas (GHG) emissions in to the biosphere. ... BC's green economy is one that is powered by green technologies and practices in every dimension of society and as such, one that generates green jobs, creates more sustainable businesses, and stimulates low-carbon investments province-wide."[91]

The United Nation's Green Economy Initiative defines "greening" an economy as the "reshaping and refocusing policies, investments and spending towards a range of sectors, such as clean technologies, renewable energies, water services, green transportation, waste management, green buildings and sustainable agriculture and forests. Greening the economy refers to the process of reconfiguring businesses and infrastructure to deliver better returns on natural, human and economic capital investments, while at the same time reducing greenhouse gas emissions, extracting and using less natural resources, creating less waste and reducing social disparities."[92]

Tacking on the goal of "reducing social disparities" is common among the definitions of green economy and is rooted in the idea that sustainability must be broadly defined to include stewarding not only natural capital, but social and human capital as well. In this context, "sustainable" jobs and a generally less exploitive approach to economics are seen as a way to rebalance inequitable social relationships.

This crops up, for example, in the definition of a "clean technology company" that appears in a report for Sustainable Development Technology Canada: "A company that is predominantly engaged in the development and marketing and/or use of its proprietary technology to deliver products and services that reduce or eliminate negative environmental impacts, *and address social needs*; while delivering competitive performance, and/or using fewer resources than conventional technologies or services" (emphasis added).[93]

The following definition of the green economy from another UN Green Economy Initiative document summarizes the presumed transformative power of the green revolution: "A Green Economy is one in which the vital links between economy, society, and environment are taken into account and in which the transformation of production processes, production and consumption patterns, while contributing to a reduction per unit in reduced waste, pollution, and the use of resources, materials, and energy, waste, and pollution emission will revitalize and diversify economies, create decent employment opportunities, promote sustainable trade, reduce poverty, and improve equity and income distribution."[94]

A more practical definition is provided by ECO Canada: the green economy is the "aggregate of all activity operating with the primary intention of reducing conventional levels of resource consumption, harmful emissions, and minimizing all forms of environmental impact. The green economy includes the inputs, activities, outputs and outcomes as they relate to the production of green products and services." The ECO Canada report goes on to identify "the top areas of opportunity in Canada within the emerging green economy [as] renewable energy and energy efficiency; buildings, retro-fitting and construction; transportation and alternative transportation; and waste recycling and waste management."[95]

The Business Case for Going Green

There are four key reasons for Canadian businesses to embrace green as the new black.

1) Externalities

First, there are the indirect costs of *not* being green. Imagine a mean-spirited factory owner. You know the stereotype: he wears a top hat, lights his cigars with $100 bills and has a big bushy mustache with errant bits of food in it. The cheapest way for him to get rid of the waste his factory produces is to dump it straight into the river (which is pretty much what used to happen not that long ago). Goodbye waste, hello profits.

Luckily, most contemporary Canadian business owners can see the bigger picture (though it often takes some prodding from concerned citizens and their governments). The bigger picture shows that, even if you don't care about the environment like our old-time factory owner, you will want to think about and adopt a greener option than dumping toxic muck into the nearest body of water because of the indirect costs (or what economists refer to as *negative externalities*). These costs could include employees who don't show up for work because the water they drink has made them sick; customers who drink the water and end up spending their money on health services rather than the widgets the factory churns out; boycotts of the factory's products by concerned citizens; and higher business taxes to help pay for all the problems caused by the pollution. In the long run, a polluted environment is not good for business. (There are also business owners who want a clean river regardless of what polluting it does or does not cost them.)

Some businesses will go ahead and pollute anyway because they decide that the benefits will still outweigh the costs. Others will pollute out of sheer ignorance. Some will cross their fingers and hope that enough businesses play by the rules that their bad behaviour will give them an advantage without completely eroding the social and environmental foundation upon which their business rests.

In a famous scene in the movie *Erin Brockovitch*, the title character (played to great effect by Julia Roberts) tells representatives from a company that denies polluting a town's water supply that the water in their drinking glasses was "brought in special" from the affected water source. The company representatives decline to drink because they know the truth. This scene illustrates why responsible environmental behaviour makes sense: barring those who move to a remote island or a secret underground bunker with a self-contained biosphere, we all have to live with the consequences of polluting our environment.

In recent years, the idea of "ecological goods and services" has started to gain acceptance. Ecological goods and services are provided free by our friendly neighbourhood environment. They include things like fresh water filtration, wild fish, fertile soil, crop pollination, beautiful vistas to recharge our souls, and clean air. They go far beyond the economic factor of production known as "land" (as in land, labour and capital) to encompass the natural processes that sustain us all.

As the concept has gained currency, so too has the idea that Canadians should perhaps include these products and services in economic equations—especially when their availability is reduced by human activity. In other words, Canadians should recognize that, even though the ecological goods and services are "free," when they hamper nature's ability to provide them, there is a cost that gets paid one way or the other. Arguably, an economy that places value on these natural products and services will benefit over an economy that recklessly depletes them.

While the costs to a specific firm may seem negligible, Canadian businesses generally understand that a pleasant, sustainable environment gives them a leg up on foreign competitors who, for example, may find it hard to attract highly skilled workers because talented people with a choice don't want to live in a polluted city. (Refer to Chapter 4 and the discussion from the Knight Frank survey of "Best Global Cities." Toronto ranks #10 overall, but only because it ranks #3 in the category of "quality of life" and natural environment.) As a result, there is a basic level of self-interest that, combined with watchful governments, has led to a minimum level of greenness among Canadian businesses.

Disagreements about whether this minimum level is sufficient are common. The point is not that Canadians have achieved all that they need to achieve, but that smart businesses know that they have a stake in a healthy environment. If they take the long view, businesses see that a healthy environment provides a tactical and strategic advantage over businesses that must deal with the adverse effects of an unhealthy environment. They also see that the short-term boost provided by ignoring environmental issues is negated by the long-term costs. For those who just want to get rich quick and get out, this does not apply. Hence, governments define and enforce a wide range of environmental rules.

The general agreement among Canadians that they shouldn't pollute does not, of course, mean that all environmental problems will go away. But as Canadian businesses think about how they can become more competitive—and how Canada will become more competitive as a result—it will pay to listen to their environmental conscience rather than the little devil on their other shoulder.

Fair enough, avoiding obvious environmental damage is a good idea from a long-term business perspective. But this does not go very far in terms of gaining a competitive edge over businesses in other advanced industrial countries where environmental standards are as high or higher than in Canada. Nor does it provide much solace to businesses that are hurting in the short-term because their competitors are skipping out on paying their environmental bills and, in turn, offering cheaper products to the very consumers who are pressuring Canadian companies to be more environmentally responsible. No one said the global economy was fair!

2) Efficiency

The second argument why Canadian businesses should go green is simple: there are potential efficiency gains to be had that can provide a competitive edge.

Take this example: a large company spends $1 million a year on paper. Someone in middle management has a bright idea and asks everybody to double-side their printouts and copies. People grumble at first about this change, but they do it and—lo and behold!—the company's paper costs go down by 25%. Small potatoes to a large company, but these changes start to add up. More cash will be available to reinvest in new equipment or machinery, which gives the company a competitive edge.

Other companies may start doing the same thing, and the advantage disappears, but the search continues for greater efficiency though green thinking. This is part of the age-old effort to get better at what you do seen through a green lens. It remains to be seen how much green efficiency can be squeezed out of the Canadian economy. Reducing everything from the amount of product packaging to the amount of power businesses use has the potential to result in a leaner and more competitive Canadian economy.

This transition, like so many others discussed in this book, requires a change of attitude and action on a massive scale. Turning the lights off when the conference room is unoccupied and belittling customers who need a plastic bag will not get the job done. Green efficiency (indeed, efficiency of all kinds) needs to become instinctual among employees at all levels of Canada's businesses. Canadians need to search out every nook and cranny of how they operate and, if they can reduce costs without compromising quality by taking a green approach, they should.

3) Reputation

What about when "going green" actually does costs more than the old way of doing things? Leaving aside the desire to be green for its own sake, a business may decide to swallow any additional cost of a more environmentally option because it pays to be *seen* as green. Indeed, maintaining a green reputation is the third reason why being green provides an economic advantage.

The idea here is that the businesses that do not to take action on environmental issues may be penalized by a global consumer marketplace and policy realm that are increasingly demanding greener processes and products. The goal is not to simply appear to be green (i.e., to engage in "greenwashing"), but to use actual green practices to win the hearts and minds of consumers, potential business partners, and the regulatory agents of governments who want a greener economy. It is the reputations of these companies that are at stake.

Jock Finlayson of the Business Council of British Columbia is observing a real shift in attitudes—one that needs to continue:

> Traditionally business leaders and environmental advocates have tended to be pit against each other. But that is changing as more industries and firms look for ways to lower energy costs, economize on resource use, and mitigate the environmental impact of their operations at all levels (resource extraction, manufacturing, transport, supply chain management, etc). In extractive industries and some parts of heavy manufacturing, there is the added challenge that firms increasingly need to maintain a social license to operate, and this demands that they be—and are seen as—responsible stewards of the environment.[96]

Too often, business interests and entrepreneurs in Canada have had knee-jerk reactions when they are confronted with environmental concerns. They've tended to dismiss these as the rants of "tree huggers" and disregard their concerns as silly and naive. But in the process, they've also missed out on some opportunities to gain efficiencies, reduce waste, cut costs and improve their social license to operate.

4) Expanding Market Potential

The fourth reason Canadian businesses should go green lies in the opportunity to capture markets for new green products and services. If, for example, Americans want bio-degradable poop bags for their dogs and are willing to pay triple for them, Canadian businesses should pay attention. (As we discussed earlier, the best way to do this would be for a Canadian firm to design and engineer the poop bags and own the biodegradable patent, rather than as the actual manufacturer.) A more serious example (though don't count out the profits to be had from expensive biodegradable poop bags!) would be selling land reclamation expertise gained from our experiences with oil sands development to jurisdictions in need of similar services.

As Roach and Ritchie argue in *The Green Grail*,

> Perhaps the most interesting opportunity for the green economy is the reality of increased energy demand in some of the world's emerging economic powers. ... This represents a massive market for green technology companies, and if western Canadian companies can be at the forefront of providing innovative and adaptable energy solutions to the billions of people living in these developing countries, the green economy could become very important.[97]

Is this a lasting "green gold rush" as former California Governor Arnold Schwarzenegger would have people believe? Can Canadians re-invigorate the weak areas of their economy by selling green products and services to the world? Will the new jobs Canada needs be green jobs? Should Canadians put all their eggs in the same green economic basket? Yes and no.

Well on his way to impoverishing himself and his family, Karl Marx envisioned a world in which humans would be free to "do one thing today and another tomorrow, to hunt in the morning, fish in the afternoon, rear cattle in the evening, criticize after dinner." For most of us, Marx's vision is marred by the need to get a job that pays the bills. So while it's fun to imagine winning the lottery or dreaming of a utopia in which Marxism actually makes sense, more practical economists, entrepreneurs, and policymakers are looking for the next source of new jobs.

The reality is that jobs come and go. When Canada was a young country, there were lots of jobs in farming. Today, giant GPS-guided combines and other technological advances mean that Canada doesn't need as many people working on the land. Similarly, lots of things used to be manufactured in Canada, but many of these jobs have gone overseas where people are willing to work for a lot less.

At the same time, new jobs were created in industries like designing videogames and selling people stuff over the Internet. But Canada needs even more new jobs to replace the ones that go elsewhere or simply disappear as technology and social change render them obsolete.

According to folks like President Obama and former California Governor Schwarzenegger, the "green economy" is where the new jobs that Americans need will be found. Many Canadians feel that this also applies to Canada. They argue that, as the green economy grows, so too will the number of people who are able to find gainful employment within it.

Sounds great, but there are a few problems with this plan.

The green economy is activity that directly improves environmental sustainability. Greater environmental sustainability is a valid goal, but it does not necessarily lead to a net gain in jobs. For example, a home builder that decides to catch the green wave by building environmentally sustainable homes is now part of the green economy, but she is still doing the same job as before, just in a greener way. As such, many green jobs will simply be replacements for non-green jobs rather than true additions to the economy. Think of a gas station worker finding employment at an electric charging station. This is a lot better than the gas station worker not finding a job at an electric charging station, but breaking even is not the same as coming out ahead.

When it comes to jobs, what Canada really needs is employment tied to an increase in overall economic activity. For example, assume that Canada starts producing a lot of solar panels for foreign customers (which is a big assumption given the competition Canada faces from the Chinese and US solar panel industries). The jobs created in the solar panel sector would be both green and net additions to the job market.

This raises a key question: how many new jobs is the green economy creating on a net basis? Is the green economy the seed from which much-needed new jobs will grow? The short answer is that we do not know because we don't have a good way of measuring the number of net jobs the green economy is creating. What we do know, however, comes from a US Department of Commerce study of the green economy in the United States. It found that green economic activity—even when you include existing things like muffler repair and bicycle manufacturing—accounts for about 2% of the overall economy.[98] Canada is not the US, but it is likely that the green economy in Canada is also relatively small.

For now, at least, the green economy is not the sea change some claim it to be, nor is it the job-creating behemoth Canada needs to keep its economy strong. Canadians will have to do a lot more than ride the green wave to economic success.

There is, however, *potential* for future growth, and Canadians should not look this gift horse (too closely) in the mouth. To the degree that good (i.e., productive, well-paying, and interesting) jobs can be created in the green economy and Canadian businesses can attract capital for, and profits from, green products and services, the green economy should be pursued. Indeed, if Canadians can position themselves as leaders in the global green economy, it may well prove to be a way for them to maintain, or even grow, their piece of the global pie.

As an emerging sector, the green economy in Canada faces a variety of challenges including a lack of venture capital and the difficulties associated with getting to the commercialization stage of product development. There are opportunities for public policy to take a proactive role, but the degree to which government should intervene is ultimately a political question embedded in the broader debate about state intervention in the economy. One thing is clear: if the green economy in Canada is to take off in a big way, more venture capital will have to be found in either the private sector or in the form of government support.

The Link Between the Green Economy and Energy

Not that long ago, the biggest criticism of using oil, gas and coal was that doing so pollutes the air and, as the 1989 Exxon Valdez oil spill demonstrated so dramatically, water and shorelines as well. These issues remain (witness the BP oil leak in the Gulf of Mexico that dominated the news in the spring of 2010). They have, however, been supplanted in large part by the "war on carbon." In the post-*An Inconvenient Truth* world, oil, gas and coal are seen as a problem because burning these releases greenhouse gases into the atmosphere that, according to many scientists, will cause widespread devastation.

Because of this, and the pervasiveness of oil, gas and coal in the global energy mix, the idea of a green economy is almost synonymous with the idea of a low-carbon (or, for some, no-carbon) economy. This is, for example, the main driver behind the Obama Administration's support of the green economy. Nonetheless, there is more to the green economy than the pursuit of lower greenhouse gas emissions. Reducing waste, stewarding the world's natural resources, preserving habitat, protecting fresh water, and a wide range of other environmental goals are central to the green economy.

With that said, because of the importance of energy to modern life and the ongoing global quest for alternatives to hydrocarbon fuels, it is difficult to imagine a definition of the green economy that does not place a premium on the shift toward a low-carbon economy. Indeed, finding "cleaner" energy sources and reducing greenhouse gas emissions have become the poster children of the green economic movement.

Going Through the Green Light

The Canadian economy does quite well at harnessing the environment and the earth's natural resources. Yet 21st century society is at odds with itself trying to balance economic growth as usual with higher respect and appreciation for the natural world. There has been progress: recycling has become commonplace, dumping industrial waste in rivers has been banned and the use of ozone-depleting aerosols has been greatly reduced. Despite these and other minor adaptations, Canada's basic economic DNA still sees only two colors: black and red. It doesn't yet recognize green—at least not broadly.

The point here is not to shame ourselves for what we have accomplished as a civilization. The modern Canadian economy and its roots in transforming the land and harvesting the earth's resources has improved living standards and life expectancy. Nonetheless, Canadians don't want to become an economic dinosaur staring into a future where they are just a bunch of bones in a museum. They have to move beyond tinkering at the margins of how their economy operates and embrace a completely different approach to how they weld our economy with the short-, medium- and long-term health of the planet.

The first thing Canadians will have to admit is that this will not be easy and it will not come without some cost. It will pay off in the long run, but like anything worth having, it may at times require some sacrifice. There will be winners and losers, and the losers are not going to be happy. If Canadians plan for this rather than think that the transition to a green future will be painless, their chances of success will be much greater.

The second thing Canadians need to understand is that one-off reactions to the crisis of the day—be it greenhouse gases, oil spills, birds being killed in wind turbines, or the disappearing rainforest—will not get the job done. Canadians need to change the basic economic equation of the 20th century in which land, labour and capital were exploited with little thought of the future, to a much more complex algorithm that incorporates the value of ecological goods and services, establishes the primacy of green creativity and innovation, and moves past the notion that "protecting" the environment is either a cost or a moral obligation. Sustainable practices must be as natural as breathing. If they are only the result of laws, guilt or religious fervour, they will always be on shaky ground and open to fierce opposition.

Thirdly, Canadians must drop the tiresome, pejorative labels such as "tree-huggers" and "corporate greed" that poison the national dialogue on the environment. As we've argued in this chapter, the business community actually has much in common with environmentalists, albeit for different reasons. But the current lack of respect and abundance of suspicion between the two groups has kept them miles apart on finding practical solutions. It's time Canadians drop the name-calling and grow up.

Canada needs business practices, investment strategies, production systems, accounting methods, entrepreneurial norms and market signals that integrate both the efficiencies that can be gained from green economics and its respect for the natural processes that sustain life. A change of this magnitude is a massive undertaking, and for this reason alone it cannot be centrally controlled. It has to happen at the level of the individual firm, investor, entrepreneur, worker, parent and teacher.

Two things make this transformation increasingly likely.

First, there are many potential financial advantages to a greener economy including lower production costs and higher profits; new jobs in the green services sector; and decreases in onerous government regulation. Canadian companies need to realize and more fully appreciate the potential efficiency gains that can be reaped by going green.

Second, Canadians know more today that they used to. Technologies are continually advancing to help solve some of the most pressing environmental issues, and new, yet-undiscovered technologies will surely emerge in the coming decade. Technology alone cannot solve all problems, nor should Canadians be looking for ways to engineer their way out of a problem without first examining their wastefulness. But technology will be a key driver to a cleaner tomorrow.

There are multiple reasons for why Canada should be leading the global economy on environmental stewardship—and economics is one of them. The next generation of Canadian entrepreneurs, investors, managers and workers needs to be much savvier about the need for, and value of, greater balance between harvesting the earth's bounty and ensuring that it continues to be bountiful.

Chapter 11

The Social Gene

"Man is by nature a social animal."
— Aristotle, Politics

We have talked a lot in this book about the Canadian economy and how to ensure that it is competitive. But we have also talked about things like education, creativity, risk-taking and innovative design because the success of the Canadian economy will depend on these things more and more. The economy, in other words, does not exist in a vacuum but is interwoven with the broader social system.

The basic argument of this chapter is that gregariousness—and lots of it—is an essential trait of the new economic animal Canada needs to become. We argue that the type of society you have determines the kind of economy you have. Even if it is the other way around, the social traits that get cultivated are critical.

If Canadians don't get the social part right, it will be like having speedboat powered by cosmopolitanism, creativity and risk-taking, but having no water in which to put it.

Nice to Meet You

The first social ingredient critical to Canada's future economic success may seem obvious: Canadians need to be out and about interacting with each other as much as possible. Lone wolf inventors, gated communities, people sequestered in their basement "media room" bunkers, angry drivers cocooned in their cars, fear, apathy, racism—basically anything that keeps people from potentially being together—are problems. They lead to a bland and unstable society. They're also problems because they undermine the creativity and innovation the Canadian economy needs. Social interaction leads to thinking about others and seeing things from different perspectives. This, in turn, leads to creativity that is "not only novel, but also useful" in a social context.[99]

Creative solutions, new product development, attracting investors, building relationships with staff, working with domestic and foreign partners—these sorts of things are critical to Canada's economic success and they all require skillful and plentiful social interaction. While brainpower is necessary, the sentiment behind "it's not *what* you know but *who* you know" is bang on. After all, the economy is a system of *exchange* and the more exchanges that take place, the better. Social interaction has all sorts of benefits including reciprocity (i.e., friendship and trust): "[a]n effective norm of generalized reciprocity is likely to be associated with dense networks of social exchange."[100]

Drawing an example from the world of pop music, even a solo artist needs a great manager, a savvy lawyer or two, some marketing staff, and so on to succeed. If people are walled off from each other by economic status, race or some other unnecessary barrier, there is less exchange—less stirring of the social gumbo. Similarly, if people are socially awkward wallflowers, they will miss out on the creative exchanges and business partnerships that make the ideas in this book come alive. In keeping with this, de Tocqueville goes so far as to call the art of association the mother of action.[101]

Canadians need to be like atoms in a particle accelerator smashing into each other and seeing what happens. The more they do this, and the more different people they do it with, the greater the chances that economic activity and the social grease that facilitates it will result. It could happen at a church. It could happen at a heavy metal concert. It could happen in line at a coffee shop, on a bike path, at a chamber of commerce luncheon, at a charity run, across the fence with a neighbour. It can't be controlled or predicted and governments can't legislate it. It has to come from the recognition that lots of interaction and community involvement is a good thing. Businesses that understand this will have an edge:

> …managers interested in fueling creativity will find it advantageous to create conditions that support prosocial motivation and perspective taking. For example, managers may directly introduce opportunities for perspective taking between employees and their clients or suppliers…, structure opportunities for employees to interact with the beneficiaries or end users of their work…, or communicate the urgency of customers' and coworkers' problems. These conditions can enhance prosocial motivation and perspective taking by enabling employees to empathize with others' needs and become more aware of the difference that their ideas can make in others' lives.[102]

Trust Me

It won't do much good if, while Canadians are out and about interacting, they conclude that they are better off avoiding each other. Hence, the second social ingredient needed to give Canada a competitive edge in the global economic race is a high degree of social trust.

As Fukuyama argues in *Trust: The Social Virtues and the Creation of Prosperity,*

> Today, having abandoned the promise of social engineering, virtually all serious observers understand that liberal political and economic institutions depend on a healthy and dynamic civil society for their vitality. "Civil society"—a complex welter of intermediate institutions, including businesses, voluntary associations, educational institutions, clubs, unions, media, charities, and churches—builds, in turn, on the family, the primary instrument by which people are socialized into their culture.... A strong and stable family structure and durable social institutions cannot be legislated into existence the way a government can create a central bank or an army. A thriving civil society depends on a people's habits, customs, and ethics—attributes that can be shaped only indirectly through conscious political action and must otherwise be nourished through an increased awareness and respect for culture.[103]

As with many of the other traits discussed in this book, Canada is starting from a solid pole position. Canadians go into business together all the time, they generally respect contracts, and corruption, while far from unknown, is not rampant. It is not quite good enough just to shake on it, but generally speaking, economic exchanges in Canada are reliable and honest. Underlying this is a society where, far more often than not, people get along. And getting along is the basis of social trust.

One way to maintain this is to embrace the social interaction noted above. Establishing and nurturing relationships—both economic and social—with a wide variety and large number of people increases understanding, fosters respect and cultivates social trust. Add to this a culture deeply rooted in respect for the rule of law, well versed in the norms and benefits of capitalism and accepting (even if grudgingly) of the rights, freedoms and responsibilities that come along with liberal democracy, and you have one heck of an economic advantage.

This means that risk-takers, for example, don't become despondent and abandon capitalism if they fail. This means that people accept the judgments of the courts rather than try to bribe their way out of trouble or appeal to friends or family members in power to make exceptions on their behalf. This means working tirelessly to ensure that liberal democracy stays healthy and does not degenerate into a system overrun with red tape, litigation, broken institutions, apathy and paternalism. People need to know that, even if they don't always agree with the decisions of their governments, that those decisions are the result of a fair process. They need to know that they are better off sticking with liberal democracy than allowing tyranny (even if it is benevolent) to seduce them with its promise of reliable trains and quick fixes.

Karl Marx was right. (Did we just say that?) If capitalism only benefits the ultra-rich and liberal democracy is manipulated into only serving the needs of those same ultra-rich, the system will break down. When Marx was writing, social trust was in short supply and class divisions pitted the peasants and workers against the aristocrats and businessmen. Things looked bad for capitalism.

In Canada and other advanced industrial democracies, an unofficial deal was struck in which the benefits of capitalism trickle down to most people most of the time. Only a few get to live in mansions or own private jets and poverty remains an issue. But overall, Canadians have it pretty good.

This is where Marx was wrong. Capitalism is a tool, not an inevitable historical force. As such, Canadians have learned how to use it to spread prosperity across the population. While more resilient than news reports make it sound in days when stock prices are down, capitalism in Canada rests on a fragile foundation. It requires the *trust* Canadians place in it and in each other. As Fukuyama argues, if social capital "is abundant, then both markets and democratic politics will thrive. ... A healthy capitalist economy is one in which there will be sufficient social capital in the underlying society to permit businesses, corporations, networks and the like to be self-organizing."[104] This maximizes not only personal freedom, but also the economic dynamism needed to compete in the knowledge economy. You may be able to jackboot people into manufacturing widgets or beguile people with government make-work projects, but you need a free and open society to enable the creativity and innovation that will propel Canada forward in the years ahead.

Some argue that countries that have government unhindered by the debates, freedoms, rights, compromises and due processes that characterize liberal democracy have an economic advantage over a place like Canada. We have heard many ask questions like the following: "Wouldn't it be great if we could make big policy decisions like they do in China without all the dilly-dallying that takes place in Canada?"

Our first response to this line of thinking is that it's worth it. We will take a free society over a dictatorship any day even it means slower economic growth. Second, the advantages of an open society compensate for its inefficiencies. This has been documented by, among others, Robert Putnam and Francis Fukuyama. Third, although China is only one example, it is worth taking a closer look at because the Middle Kingdom's economy is on everyone's mind these days. What is interesting about China's economic rise (remember when the mover and shaker in Asia was Japan?) is that it has not been the state directed elements that have driven China's growth, but the *loosening* of the state's grip on free enterprise.

It's important to point out that we are advocating for neither small government nor large government. We leave the question of how large the state's role in the economy should be to others. What we have observed, however, is that public policy (i.e., the things governments choose to do or not to do) is a critical factor in the economy and, in turn, if policymakers and policymaking are seen as inherently suspect or inevitably wrongheaded, the economic effects are negative. Even if it is decided that minimal state involvement is best, government's role in the economy has to have legitimacy in the eyes of citizens and stakeholders. This is why apathy and cynicism undermine not just civic institutions, but also the economic edge a healthy democracy and engaged citizenship create. Canadians need appropriate skepticism about government and informed policy alternatives are always worth articulating and debating. This should not, however, deteriorate into general animosity toward anything coming from government. The result of such animosity is policy inertia, or worse, policy failure.

The more Canadians can do to foster trust and the social capital it builds, the better. As with social interaction, you can't legislate social trust into being and, while specific prescriptions such as encouraging people to join bowling leagues or teaching more civics classes in school may help, it comes down to the willingness of individual Canadians to actively earn the trust of one another. On the negative side of the ledger, Canadians need to avoid ripping each other off or marginalizing those who are different. On the positive side, Canadians need to have empathy for one another and appreciate the value of good relationships. The new Canadian economic animal has to "get this" on an instinctual level.

Where are you from?

In Chapter 7, we argue that cosmopolitanism works best when it is grounded in strong communities at home—places people want to come to and come back to. People will make their own choices about where to live based on all sorts of factors, but the more alluring Canadian communities are, the more likely it will be that they will attract the talented workers (and good citizens) Canada's economy needs.

Our urging of greater cosmopolitanism and living abroad is not meant to be a permanent exodus of Canadians. Rather, the goal is for Canada to become a globally recognized hub of economic and social action. Fortunately, a high level of social interaction and social trust are the main building blocks of the strong and interesting communities that will draw more of the world to Canada and keep members of the Canadian Diaspora yearning for home.

People will go to undesirable places for a job if the pay is high enough or if they have no other economic options, but generally speaking, they don't want to live in weak communities. They like safety, friendly neighbours, things to do, shared values, and a sense that people care about one another.

There are lots of practical ways to ensure that Canadian communities are strong and vibrant. For example, the work of people like Dan Burden (Co-Founder and Executive Director of the Walkable and Livable Communities Institute) shows that being able to get around on foot and run into people is important. Inspiring architecture and public spaces are needed as well as strong support for arts and entertainment options.

True, there is a debate about the role government should play on behalf of citizens to ensure the availability of artistic outlets that struggle to survive on their own, but regardless of where you draw this line, it is ultimately up to people, not government, to engage with and support the arts. Simply put, if you value artistic expression and local entertainment options either for you or for others (e.g., to inspire and educate your kids), put your money where your mouth is by getting out there and supporting it. You will be happier and your community will be better equipped to not only compete with other communities in the race to attract talented workers but also to inspire the creative thinking and innovative practices that are the secret to Canada's future economic success.

A healthy nonprofit sector, volunteerism, green spaces, affordable housing, and solid infrastructure are all key elements of strong communities. (Sunshine and beaches don't hurt either, but you have to work with what you have.) The task at hand is to encourage more of these things. To this end, it is important to remember that the economy is a marathon, not a sprint, and the short-term costs of investing in community will have big payoffs in the long-term.

Richard Florida has done much to popularize the idea that the knowledge economy needs creative people and that creative people like a certain sort of place. They like "creative centers" that "provide the integrated eco-system or habitat where all forms of creativity—artistic and cultural, technological and economic—can take root and flourish."[105] Even in a globalized, hyperlinked world, *place* matters. This is a fundamentally important insight that often gets lost amid the push for short-term gains and an oversimplified interpretation of what it means that capital can move anywhere. The fact that capital can move anywhere does not mean that it doesn't care where it goes. On the contrary, the fact that it is mobile means that it can pick and choose where it wants to go and take into consideration the underlying strengths of a place such as its stock of social capital and ability to seduce the skilled labour smart capital needs to maximize its returns.

It's unfortunate, however, that Florida dubbed creative people the "creative class" because the last thing Canadians need is more class divisions in their communities. More importantly, it obscures the fact that *everyone* has the potential to be a creative person. It's doubly unfortunate that Florida bases his recipe for creative centers on input from his creative class. The unsurprising result is a narrow definition of what makes a community attractive to creative people. A cool music scene and people who are hip have always been attractive to young people. The real trick is to infuse Canada's communities with a *broad* array of physical and cultural amenities rather than focusing on just one version of what "artists" tend to like. If you get too specific and try to boil down successful communities to a Bohemian index or some other measure, you risk alienating creative people who do not fit the stereotype of "the artist." In addition, the specific things people want tend to change over time. Nightlife is typically more important to a twenty-something than a fifty-something (exceptions prove the rule), but both may be highly creative workers in Canada's knowledge economy. Despite its limitations, Florida's work is extremely valuable because it gets people thinking about the importance of place and the role played by communities in supporting and shaping Canada's economic future and the role of creativity within that future.

The Tall Tree Has Deep Roots

Calgary (which happens to be our hometown) provides an interesting case study of the value of thinking about the economic importance of community. Calgary is a happening place economically. Driven by the oil and gas sector, the city is a boomtown overrun with construction, new money, malls and good jobs. Not everyone is an oil baron, indeed many Calgarians know what it's like to wonder where their next meal is coming from, but relatively speaking, Calgary is an economic success. Despite this, many Calgarians have noticed that the city sometimes seems like it is still a frontier town. The city sometimes feels like a *temporary* place that could have tumbleweeds rolling through it at any moment.

Part of this—but only part—can be explained by the periodic economic busts that are rooted in the same oil and gas sector that fuels the city's booms. When the money dries up, the prospectors tend to go home. The boom-and-bust cycle does not, however, fully explain the temporary feeling of the city. The full explanation lies in how Calgarians perceive their community.

The positive side of all this is the famous "can do" attitude that pervades the business and philanthropic sector in Calgary. People on the frontier are not weighed down by atrophied social structures; there are too many new faces and new opportunities to follow the dictates of the old guard. You don't have to be the son or daughter from the so-and-so family to make a name for yourself.

The negative side is the sense of fleetingness. Many of the buildings in Calgary, for example, are utilitarian and have an uninspired, temporary feel. The reality is that you need office or retail space fast and you may not be here next year, so why invest in fancy extras? It is also hard to miss the fact that a lot of the current residents are here to make some money and then go "back home" or retire someplace "nice." The unnecessary and misleading minute-by-minute reports of the price of oil add to the feeling that the whole thing is a house of cards that could fall down at any time.

Nonetheless, many Calgarians feel a strong sense of attachment to the city. Community spirit is strong and many people who come for a job stay for other reasons. Jobs or no jobs, the city would not have posted a net gain of over 400,000 people to its population since the mid-1990s if it wasn't a nice place to live. And it is normal and healthy for people to come and go from cities—this is after all the nature of a cosmopolitan society. It is also better to go where the jobs are than it is to prop up faltering local economies (hard as this is for the residents of communities in economic freefall to hear).

When Calgarians bring up the concern that their city sometimes feels like a traveling circus that could pack up and move on at any time, they are highlighting the importance of place and community. They are recognizing that these things matter and that they require effort to achieve and maintain. They fight against the boom-bust cycle by putting down roots and investing in the city. They work hard to promote its charms and to fix its flaws because they don't just work in Calgary—they *live* there and they plan on *staying* there.

The lesson to take away from this is that many Canadian cities, for similar and different reasons, are facing what Calgary is facing: the need to invest in communities in the midst of uncertain economic times. The economic rollercoaster ride that Calgary has always been on highlights the corrosive power of global economic forces on community and the need for conscious and concerted action to counteract this. A place like Calgary can compete in the creative economy—be this in addition to its resource economy or as a replacement for it when it can no longer play its part as the city's economic engine—but it has to make sure that it gets the community piece right. Economics is a harsh science because economic forces like commodity prices and outsourcing manufacturing to lower cost jurisdictions don't care about people and communities. That's the beauty of knowledge jobs, creative entrepreneurial initiatives, design work and high end manufacturing—they can be located pretty much anywhere and they will be naturally drawn to strong communities.

Imagine the elderly Shaolin monk in an old episode of *Kung Fu* with David Carradine saying "the tall tree has deep roots." This applies perfectly to the future economic success of Canadian cities and towns. If they have the deep roots in the form of social trust, community engagement and a high quality of life, they will have a better chance of hoping on, and staying on, the creative economy bandwagon.

Social Butterflies

As we went through our initial list of things we felt were going to be critical to Canada's economic future, it struck us that they all rely on a certain type of social profile. If Canadians don't trust each other, how are they going to go into business together? And if they can't trust each other, how are they going to trust foreigners and become more cosmopolitan? If they are sequestered from one another, how are they going to take advantage of the creativity and innovation that comes along with social interaction? If they are an inward looking bunch, how will they create the interesting and supportive communities to which the world's talented people will want to come? If they think that every politician is a crook and every bureaucrat incompetent, how will they develop and implement effective public policy? If they feel that capitalism is a crime, how will they move further up the value chain? If they fear change and failure, how will they innovate? If they freeze in the headlights of environmental challenges or if they don't care at all about being green, how will they steward their natural capital? If they don't give as much as they get, how will they avoid the social erosion and soullessness that not only hamstrings the economy, but threatens Canada's quality of life in general? If they give up on democracy, how will they have the freedom to improve the economy?

It was clear that there are a lot of social factors that are simply not conducive to the development of the competitive economy we envision. This is why the new entrepreneur that will embody the changes we suggest has to be a distinctly social animal. The new entrepreneur has to instinctively understand that there is more to the economy that the next quarter's profit or loss. She has to be a community builder as much as she is a wealth creator. She has to be a citizen as much as an employer. She has to be a friend and a collaborator as much as she is a leader and maverick. The new entrepreneur is someone you'd want to meet at a party. He has seen the world, but he loves his home here in Canada. The new entrepreneur is definitely a people person.

At its root, all economic activity is social activity. Hence, a diverse, fair, friendly and peaceful society is better for an economy than a repressed, unjust, isolating and violent society. In the short-term, dictatorships can grow an economy through force, but the underlying social landmines will eventually go off and derail things. The rule of law, a relative lack of corruption, general prosperity, guaranteed rights and freedoms, relatively low crime rates and peaceful relations internally and with its neighbours all give Canada a huge economic advantage.

The main reason why Canada's natural resources have been able to drive overall economic prosperity and the development of a mature service economy rather than merely enriching a few is the democratic nature of Canadian society. This is why discovering oil in a country where exploitation is the norm is not usually good news for the people, whereas it was (and is) good news for Canadians.

Writers such as Francis Fukuyama and Robert Putnam have highlighted the economic importance of social capital. The more people interact with each other, understand each other and trust each other, the more likely they are to successfully work together on economic projects. If you think your neighbour is going to rip you off, you are unlikely to start a risky business venture with her. Similarly, because government plays such a large role in the economy through everything from taxes and regulations to business subsidies and Crown corporations, a lack of trust or satisfaction with political institutions is detrimental to economic competitiveness and growth. You have to trust not only your neighbour, but the folks running the government as well.

In addition, creativity, innovation and new ventures require people to share ideas, enthusiasm and capital. Canadians need to be running into each other, spending time together and working together. The lonely inventor in his basement is not a good model for economic growth. Collaboration is critical.

How can Canadians encourage this gregariousness? As with so much else discussed in this book, it is up to us as individuals, parents, friends, businesses partners, colleagues, thought leaders, community activists, voters, coaches, teachers, mentors, confidants, advisors and neighbours to embrace it, encourage it, and, as much as possible, "just do it."

Canada has a head start in this area, but Canadians can't be complacent. They need to increase their lead and cultivate social interaction, community, familiarity, trust, and collaboration, all of which is required for Canadians to take more risks, translate creativity into commercial ventures and be leading players on the world stage. Just as Michael Jordan did not stop at one championship, Canadians have to strive to have a society that is the stuff of legend.

Government cannot do if for us, and there is no magic pill that will make it happen. It's incumbent upon each of us to either act or not. Pogo said that we have met the enemy and he is us. Well, we have also met the solution, and he us, too.

Chapter 12

The New Canadian Entrepreneur

> "...creation is also an act of destruction. To create something new, you also have to tear down conventional ways of thinking."
> — Gregory Berns, neuroscientist

Traditional economics teaches us that businesses—and the wealth they create—depend on the combination of three essential things known as the factors of production: land, labour and capital. The field of economics as it has been taught for most of the 20th century is essentially the study of how humans have combined the factors of production (supply) in ways that try to satisfy human desires (demand) within the economy.

But the land-labour-capital troika of production misses a key ingredient: ideas. The combination of land, labour and capital can produce nothing without an idea originating in an entrepreneur's mind. It is the idea of how to combine fertile soil, seeds and water that produces wheat. It is the idea of how to combine clay, water and a spinning wheel that produces an attractive piece of pottery. It is the idea of how to combine wood, steel, glass and a plot of land in a subdivision that produces a new home.

Unlike land, labour or capital, the ideas that originate from the human mind face no scarcity. There is absolutely no limit to the number of ideas that can flow from our imaginations. And since all wealth originates with ideas, it is quite fortunate and encouraging that ideas are indeed limitless.

Good ideas are often the forgotten piece of the puzzle in our attempts to generate wealth, economic growth and productivity. Greg Ip, a Canadian-born economist who worked as a journalist for *The Globe and Mail*, *The Wall Street Journal* and now *The Economist*, writes: "In the long-run, a country becomes rich or stagnates depending on whether it has the right mix of people, capital and ideas. Get these fundamentals right, and the short-run gyrations seldom matter."[106]

So if ideas are responsible for finding new ways to combine land, labour and capital in ways that create wealth, it follows that the recipe for Canada's prosperity in the 21st century must involve strategies for coming up with new ideas. Given this, the new Canadian entrepreneur that we envision embodies the notion that *ideas create wealth*.

Who is the New Canadian Entrepreneur?

It's a mistaken belief that entrepreneurs are a special breed of person. True, not all of us have the ambition or energy to start a new software company from scratch. But if we are willing to broaden the scope of the term "entrepreneur" to include anyone who is willing to add value to the economy through the application of an idea, it becomes clear that almost all of us have at least the potential to be entrepreneurial.

An entrepreneur in this broader sense is a mid-level manager in a large multinational corporation who identifies a creative way to process invoices more quickly that, in turn, saves the company money. An entrepreneur is an entry-level server in a restaurant who notices patrons requesting certain types of food, which sparks an idea in his mind for a new menu item. An entrepreneur is a senior VP in a niche manufacturing company who acts on her instinct to build business connections with customers in India. An entrepreneur is a recent high school graduate who, after spending a year in China, returns to Canada with a business idea involving the millions of Canadians living abroad.

Granted, not everyone may feel like an entrepreneur. There are a lot of occupations that just don't yield themselves to creative improvement—at least not on the surface. A lot of these jobs are low-skilled and fairly labour intensive, and many are considered quite menial. It would be rather ignorant to tell a custodial worker to "be more creative" in the way he cleans a toilet, or to suggest to a French fry cook that some international experience would serve her well.

There are three responses to this. The first is that, while some types of jobs are menial, most people will not do the same job forever. Many Canadians have at some point in their teens or young adult years worked at entry level positions, doing jobs such as bagging groceries, working in convenience stores, delivering pizza or mowing lawns. As young workers, we learn important skills while at these positions that should not be underestimated, such as the importance of showing up to work on time, how to accept orders from superiors and how to work in teams and serve customers. But many entry-level workers will eventually move on to other positions—ones which may require more creativity.

Second, even if a particular person remains in the same industry for his or her entire career, they are likely to end up in a more supervisory role in the future. Someone whose first job is cleaning carpets may end up supervising a cleaning crew or managing a carpet cleaning franchise. It is not much of a stretch to suggest that creativity, innovation and a more cosmopolitan attitude are important in these roles.

Third, even for the many Canadians who may always work at so called menial jobs—either intentionally or out of necessity—we believe that there is still value in bringing a creative attitude to the workplace each day. They may never come up with a ground-breaking new way to flip a hamburger or shovel a driveway, but there really is no job too small or too menial that it cannot be improved with a good idea.

In this way, we think that the suggestions offered in this book are really for every Canadian, regardless of income level, educational attainment or work history. The principles are applicable to those in the business world, to those in the volunteer sector and to those who work inside the home for no direct pay. Not all of the ideas generated are going to improve the financial bottom line of a big corporation or dramatically improve Canada's international economic competitiveness (although some will do so), but if they make someone's day more productive, more fulfilling or even just more fun, then they are worth pursuing. When added all together, the end result is a stronger Canadian economy.

Cumulative Effects

Some critics may question the effectiveness of any of these ideas in helping boost the economy. You can almost hear the naysayers: "You mean to tell me that if I visit an art gallery I'll be a more creative worker? Or that if my daughter is a risk-taker, her business idea will revolutionize the economy? Ha! What have you been smoking?"

It's a fair enough criticism, but it misses the point that none of the suggestions offered in this book are meant to be applied in isolation and none will have instant effects. The new Canadian entrepreneur is not just one person—it's an attitude that has to pervade our entire culture. It's like a snowflake: on its own, there are few things more feeble and useless. It's only a fragile, six-sided crystal of ice fluttering harmlessly to the ground. Individually it is practically meaningless. But few Canadians would doubt the power of those snowflakes taken together, such as in the awesomeness of a blizzard or avalanche or the stunning beauty of a snow-capped mountain. It's the cumulative effect that we are after.

If we all take some personal responsibility in our daily work and careers—finding ways to be more creative, innovative, risk-taking, failure-tolerant, outward looking, efficient and community-oriented—we can transform the Canadian economy into a 21st century global economic power player. But it's a team sport. The result will be—has to be—greater than the sum of the parts.

The Ten Key Characteristics of the New Canadian Entrepreneur

So what are the characteristics of the new Canadian entrepreneur? What attitudes and habits will be cultivated by those willing to help transform Canada's economy so it can thrive in the evolving international economy? And what practical steps can each of us take to be part of the solution? The following traits and suggestions are drawn from the preceding six chapters and provide a good summary of the attributes each of us needs to embody.

1) The new Canadian entrepreneur actively seeks to become more creative and takes concrete actions on ideas that have value.

As mentioned in Chapter 6, creativity is a word that comes with a lot of baggage—and it's one that's just as likely to be met with derision as with respect. Perhaps because it has been overused by many economic development gurus, or maybe because it smacks of being a motherhood statement, the term needs some clarification.

A creative person is one who *purposely* tries to look at a problem or a situation in a new way. Creativity is not the same as the capacity for imagination. To actually be creative, you have to get off your butt and do something. So, one of the traits of a creative person is the willingness to take action on an idea, an impulse or a hunch. In the world of art, it involves finding a way to express some aspect of the human condition. In the world of business, it involves finding a way to make money, keep people employed, be more productive, attract customers, design a product, sell a service and so on. When applied with care, creativity is useful in all sectors of the economy, but it is particularly important at the upper end of the value chain where we believe Canadian businesses need to be perched. Innovation can help us make better widgets and harvest resources in better ways and it can help us succeed in the knowledge economy and services sector—the very areas in which the new Canadian economic animal has the greatest potential to thrive.

The precise actions taken will depend, of course, on the situation and the idea. For a business person, imagining a new venture with a Brazilian supplier is easy. But a creative person acts on it. This could mean taking a trip to Brazil to do some reconnaissance or even something as simple as picking up the phone and making a call to a friend who has experience working in Brazil—experience obtained because of the friend's cosmopolitan outlook. The initial step may be small, but it needs to be a step or else the creativity is confined to the realm of imagination.

If everyone has the ability to be creative, what are some techniques by which to cultivate an attitude of creativity and, in turn, a truly creative economy?

The first thing to recognize is that it may not come easily or immediately. It's like physical exercise: if you tell an out-of-shape person to take up jogging, the first attempt at running could end in one or two blocks of misery. If after those few blocks, the jogger decides to pack in the running shoes for good, he'd be right in complaining "That didn't do a lick of good." But regular and repeated exercise *will* help. Becoming more creative involves a similar process. It's a discipline. You have to engage in creative activities regularly and intentionally.

Many of us have experienced mental blocks. It could be while trying to solve some problem at work or writing a bio for an online dating service. The ideas just don't seem to be coming and the harder we try to generate an idea, the more hopeless it feels. The trick at this point is to jolt the brain out of one kind of thought process by introducing something completely new and unfamiliar.

Here are some activities that could help kick-start creativity. They may seem almost too simple to be useful, but if you are intentional about it, they can be quite effective. We've separated them into easy, medium and advanced in terms of how much energy they require:

EASY

Read something different. If you regularly read only business and current affairs magazines, flip through a magazine on knitting, or puppies or martial arts. You don't need to enjoy the magazine, but spend some time perusing the articles. Pay attention to the way it's presented and how it's different from what you're used to. The idea is to surprise the mind with unfamiliar stimuli.

Take a different route to work or school. It doesn't matter that it isn't the quickest route. Routines can be good for many reasons, but sometimes slipping out of routine momentarily can make the mind pay more attention to what it sees.

MEDIUM

Find a type of art form that you haven't seen before, such as an opera, a rock concert or a conceptual art exhibit. You don't have to pick something that will torture you, but try to identify something that you'd never normally see. Again, pay attention to what makes it different from your regular world.

Unless you already do this as a matter of parenting or otherwise, make a point of spending time with a child under the age of five. This is when the world of imagination and creativity are at a fever pitch. Play with the child even if it is just for a few minutes. Don't just watch the child, but engage with the child and try to enter into his or her world of imagination.

ADVANCED

> Volunteer some time to a nonprofit organization that is outside your usual frame of reference. Working with the staff, volunteers and clients toward a common goal will poke all sorts of areas of your brain that have been dormant.
>
> Take up a specific creative pursuit. This could be anything from writing a story or making a collage of old photographs to pulling out the instrument you played back in school or taking dance classes. The point is to purposefully activate the creative parts of your brain.

These are just a few simple suggestions that offer the mind the chance to see something new, and in that way jolt the brain out of its regular thought compartments. It's shock therapy without the electricity and pain. It does take an intentional effort; however, if you're willing to try, you may be surprised by the positive effects on your mind over time.

Stepping back and looking at this from an economy-wide perspective, the theory is that the increased flow of creative juices will spill over into the workplace, education system and social sphere and, by so doing, create the conditions for a smarter, nimbler and generally more competitive Canadian economy. With that said, we recognize that the ideas above barely scratch the surface of how to become more creative and that changing Canada's economic DNA to make the economy more creative will require action on the part of parents, educators, employers and community leaders. Our point is that the new Canadian entrepreneur must have a genetic code that triggers creative action and links it to economic pursuits. The more creativity at play in our economy (as opposed to the narrow idea of a creative economy generating specific creative outputs) the better.

2) The new Canadian entrepreneur supports the arts and finds ways to expand her thinking and creativity through the arts.

Many Canadians already enjoy a wide range of artistic pursuits, either as artists or as spectators. Canadian cities have active theatre scenes, museums, musical venues, comedy clubs, galleries, dance studios, public sculptures, libraries, film production companies and other opportunities for artistic expression and viewing. The new Canadian entrepreneur is an active participant on both sides of the stage; she is both an artist and a patron.

For our purposes, artists include everyone from a middle aged repairman playing guitar in his basement to a professional ballet dancer. The phrase "the arts" makes it sound like only people who attended Julliard or who go to the opera are part of the arts scene, but this is far too narrow and patronising of a definition. We should not get bogged down in answering what counts as art. A reality TV show may have just as much right to be called art as a painting in the National Gallery. We are not saying that the educational benefits of a group of junior high students watching *The Jersey Shore* would be as great as an outing to see *Carmen* or hear Mozart played by a symphony orchestra. We are also not saying that passively watching a TV show is equivalent to supporting the arts—we have to be active participants and supporters of a range of artistic outlets and we need to make sure this happens at a local level (i.e., where it can be experienced first hand not just over the tube or the web). The point rather, is that art is in the eye of the beholder and we should not belittle the creative impulses and benefits of, for example, jamming with your buddies in the garage or hanging a child's finger painting masterpiece on the fridge.

In keeping with this, the new entrepreneur will not view the arts as something only "artists" do or something only to do during leisure time. Rather, she will consider artistic pursuits to be a vital part of the economy because they boost our creative abilities and, in turn, our business acumen. She'll recognize that the arts provide the chance for people to expand their minds, to see the world in new ways, to better understand each other and to open channels of creativity that will ultimately result in a more productive workforce, better products and services and a competitive edge in the international economy. A vibrant arts scene also helps build great cities and communities—the kind of places that are attractive to those international workers that Canadian businesses and universities are trying desperately to attract.

No matter how well an argument can be made for public (i.e., tax dollar) support for the arts, opposition will rage. At any level of government, revenue is scarce and tax dollars precious (or at least they should be seen as such by those we elect to raise and spend them); demands for infrastructure, health care, education and policing always seem to take priority over funding of the arts, much to the chagrin of artists and art organizations. While we believe that public funding of the arts is appropriate, we appreciate the fact that tax dollars are not infinite and will not, and should not, do the job alone.

The traditional alternative has been for artists to seek corporate donors or sponsors. For the most part, businesses in Canada have done a fairly good job of supporting the arts; however, we do not think the business community should be left to do all of the heavy lifting any more than government.

There is a third way to support the arts—one which doesn't require a dime of tax revenue or another pitch to a corporate donation committee: Canadians can support the arts themselves with their own personal spending.

One of the big complaints raised by fiscal conservatives who do not like to see tax dollars going to support the arts is that, if there is no audience to make it economically viable, why are we wasting tax dollars on it? While we don't fully agree with this position, there is an undeniable logic to it.

The solution is to *create* a market for it. If enough Canadians—the new entrepreneurs—invest a bit more of their time and money in the arts, it would go a long way in making them economically viable on their own. Most of us like the idea of our cities having major museums, art galleries, theatre groups and music venues, but if we never take time to visit them, should we be surprised when they have to go cap-in-hand to governments and businesses for money?

Here are some practical ideas for how the new Canadian entrepreneur, and the companies they work for/own, can support the arts:

→ Make it a point to see one piece of art (a play, a concert, an art show, etc.) each month. Find someone to do it with and make a commitment. Buy a season ticket for a theatre company, for example. Instead of sitting at home watching reruns of *Two and a Half Men,* take in a blues band or comedy act. Try to find an art form with which you may be unfamiliar.

→ Companies could encourage their employees to take in the arts as part of "professional development." Companies that see the value in fostering a creative culture within their office may want to organize a team building afternoon where the whole office goes to a museum or attends the ballet. It may not be what everyone is interested in ("Why can't I just go home?") so it shouldn't be viewed as free time. It should be considered an investment in human resources.

→ Companies could also consider programs that enable underprivileged children to attend arts events.

→ The new Canadian entrepreneur will value the teaching of the arts in schools and will activity discourage school boards from chopping arts subjects because they are "unnecessary." Traditionally, art in school has been treated as superfluous. This thinking needs to change. Art is every bit as important to the development of a child's mind and thinking patterns as are the sciences and math. In fact, it is the child who learns to think with his or her entire mind—both the logical, linear brain as well as the emotional, relational brain—that will succeed in the future.

3) The new Canadian entrepreneur has lived abroad and values employees and business partners who have lived abroad.

Notwithstanding the contributions of First Nations, Canada is a country built by immigrants. And indeed Canadians share a wide variety of cultural and ethnic traditions which make for a rich, vibrant country. Toronto is often recognized as being one of the most multicultural cities on the planet! Despite Canada's rich multicultural heritage, however, Canadians are not especially connected to the rest of the global economy—or at least not as much as some of their competitors are.

The new Canadian entrepreneur will explore the possibilities of living abroad, preferably for an extended period. Ideally, she will return and bring back to Canada a wealth of new ideas, perspectives and attitudes that will enrich our domestic economy. Some may immediately claim that moving to another country is too expensive and impractical. Jobs, mortgages, kids in school and dozens of other barriers make it practically impossible to just pick up and move. But is it really that difficult? There are examples of people who have done exactly this. Some employers are willing to consider extended leaves of absences for employees, especially valuable ones that they'd like to keep. Making the case that you will be returning to your job in six month's time with a richer life experience may not be as difficult as it seems.

However, it is far easier to spend a year or two living abroad when you are young, unattached, and still relatively unencumbered by jobs and mortgages. This is why encouraging young people to do an overseas experience (OE) makes sense. So far, the OE is not an integral part of Canadian culture. While it's always possible to find some young Canadians who have done exactly this, it remains the exception rather than the norm. A key challenge here is to make sure that doing an OE does not become common only among the wealthy. If we put our heads together, Canadians from all socio-economic backgrounds should be able to work abroad if they choose. This will require building resources into the education system (e.g., information on how to do an OE) and developing financial mechanisms that can assist young people to get to another country and find a job (e.g., travel loans akin to student loans and businesses focused on OE job searches and the like).

Individual experiences may vary, but our suspicion is that many Canadian parents of young adults would activity discourage (even prohibit!) the idea of moving abroad. A back-packing trip across Europe for a couple of months would be tolerated in most cases, and certainly there is value in that kind of experience. But, as we've argued elsewhere, this is not the same thing as *living* abroad—getting a job, finding a place to rent, making social connections, paying bills, visiting a doctor or dentist...these are the kinds of experiences you get only when you actually live somewhere for an extended period.

It's one thing to live abroad or encourage your kids to do so, but quite another to actually value and utilize the experience in the economy. If employers and educators do not recognize time spent working abroad as an asset that they can use, OEs still make sense, but the economic punch they can deliver will be much weaker than it could be. The new entrepreneur sees the value in working with people who have lived abroad. Sometimes the benefits will be immediate and clear (e.g., a business partner who has brought back knowledge and contacts relevant to a new venture or a worker who is able to develop better rapport with customers from the same area where she worked abroad). And sometimes—perhaps most of the time—the benefits will be intangible at first, but there nonetheless (e.g., a more confident employee who is just a wee bit more creative because they have seen how things work elsewhere in the world).

Even bad experiences can be useful if only to highlight how good life is in Canada.

4) The new Canadian entrepreneur encourages foreign students, entrepreneurs and academics to come to Canada.

Also as part of developing a more cosmopolitan society, Canadians need to embrace a more welcoming attitude toward foreigners who are looking to Canada for opportunities.

This issue gets complex very quickly as critics point to issues of terrorism and refugees taking advantage of Canadian generosity. But these concerns need to be balanced with the fact that Canada needs international migration just to maintain its population. More to the point, Canada's economy needs to attract the best and brightest students, business entrepreneurs and scholars in the world if it is to remain competitive in the global economy.

Sponsoring foreign high school students to come study in Canada and vice versa is one method. Increasing the efforts and capacity of Canada's universities, colleges and polytechnics to attract foreign students and faculty is another.

As for attracting foreign businesses and investment, the new Canadian entrepreneur will welcome the opportunities that this brings. Supporting efforts like Startup Visa Canada, which seeks to streamline the process for foreign entrepreneurs to set up shop in Canada, is one way to do so. If the Canadian government and provincial nominee programs receive a loud and clear message that the business community wants to see more foreign entrepreneurs coming to Canada, the more likely we are to see change at the policy level. The wealth of ideas, connections and entrepreneurial energy foreign business people could bring to Canada is certain to enliven the economy. Rather than seeing them as unwelcomed competitors, the new Canadian entrepreneur will jump on the opportunities to do joint business ventures with these newcomers, because she will understand the benefits that new ideas and approaches can bring.

5) The new Canadian entrepreneur sees the international economy as her natural habitat.

In addition to supporting working abroad through some combination of doing it, facilitating it for others and valuing the results, and on top of welcoming the world's students, teachers, researchers, immigrants and investors to Canada with open arms, the new Canadian entrepreneur will always have at least one eye fixed on the international economy. She will be as likely to partner with a foreigner as with a Canadian. She will see the potential for selling all sorts of products and services to people in other countries. She will be inspired by foreign competition and not be content to be a big fish in a protected Canadian pond.

On the domestic front, she will recognize the value of the diversity of Canadian society and harness this to her economic pursuits. Whether it is Canada's Aboriginal peoples, immigrant communities, urban bohemians or rural folk, the new entrepreneur will see that this mix of backgrounds, perspectives, skills and experiences is a tremendous asset.

6) The new Canadian entrepreneur is a risk-taker.

Understanding the difference between healthy *fear* and unhealthy *anxiety* in making business decisions will differentiate the successful from the unsuccessful. Canadians need to purposely and intentionally become more willing to take on risk. To allow anxiety to paralyze a business decision will only result in Canada's economy falling further behind.

Becoming better at risk-taking is like physical exercise. No book or course on physical fitness in the world will improve your health until you actually put on your running shoes (or yoga pants, or swim suit or skis.) and do something! Taking a chance in the business world—even if there is some risk involved—is the same.

But to be clear, we are not advocating reckless business ventures and half-baked ideas that are sure to end in financial ruin. This is where a healthy *fear* of losing money is a valuable trait. The new Canadian entrepreneur will be willing to test her business idea on friends, family members and colleagues—and she will ask for brutally honest answers (see the next section).

Some ideas just really shouldn't be pursued with even just 10 cents of capital. But some ideas—even if they seem nutty—may hold a nugget of promise. Part of the candid feedback from friends and colleagues will be to ask for critical yet positive messages. Is there a business idea here? What are the flaws? What are the possibilities? Can the idea be tweaked in a way that will improve the probability of success?

All of these principles hold true even if it is not a new business you are starting, but rather an idea for a new process or product within an existing company. Speak up at meetings. Take a risk and suggest things. Forcefully put aside the fear of being shot down by coworkers or even your managers. Ultimately, though, there are no sure bets. Act with rational caution, but act. Do something risky, even if that risk involves nothing more than overcoming shyness or fear of being mocked by starting the discussion: "I've got an idea…"

Similarly, when the new entrepreneur is on the other side of the table and looking to invest, she will seek out and act positively toward creative ideas and be open to supporting risky ventures. Canadian investors can't always play it safe and expect strong returns. Both the Canadian and global economy can be dangerous places for capital, but hiding out in safe havens will not give Canadians the stakes in the innovative wealth creation vehicles needed to keep the economy strong in the years ahead. The new entrepreneur gets this and judiciously supports good ideas so they can be commercialized and start creating wealth and jobs for Canadians.

7) The new Canadian entrepreneur is not afraid to offer candid opinions and honest advice, but does so in a way that encourages creative ideas and identifies potential.

Boardroom discussions and brain storming sessions are often dominated by negativity and naysaying. Like Patrick Finn describes in Chapter 9, we've become trained to be idea ninjas with a reflex to punch and kick down every new idea that arises because it may not fit within our fixed scope of understanding. We do this in the name of critical thinking, but the end result is economic inertia.

The other mistake we sometimes make lies at the opposite end of the spectrum and stems from our overly polite Canadian social norms. Too often, when presented with an idea—even a really terrible idea—we say nothing. We smile and nod and don't want to be viewed as a trouble maker. In these situations, silence is affirming—and it can be financially deadly.

The new Canadian entrepreneur won't be afraid to speak up when asked for feedback on an idea, but will do so in a way that is honest, frank and positive. If the idea is truly terrible, there are ways to say that without destroying the esteem of the person who voiced it. This is not to say that we should sugar-coat all of our comments and feedback. Firmness and honesty are valuable, but of equal value is encouraging an atmosphere that allows people to throw ideas out on the table. Creativity demands this.

The creation of a secure environment for ideas is linked to risk-taking. If we want people to take more risks—even if it is just suggesting an idea in a meeting—we have to create a secure environment. Most of us, if we are honest about it, are actually rather shy and even a bit insecure. This can be especially true of young employees who have just joined a corporate team—the ones from which corporate managers *say* they want creative ideas. They are still finding their feet, testing themselves and their ideas. After a few meetings in which they are shot down in flames in front of peers and managers, their creative idea capacities are damaged—often beyond repair.

The new Canadian entrepreneur will purposely set aside knee-jerk negativity, and will replace it with positive, honest and frank feedback. She will assess the new idea she confronts with an open mind.

8) The new Canadian entrepreneur wants to be at the top of the economic value chain.

We are, of course, describing tendencies that will be more or less manifest in Canadians at different points their lives and depending on their circumstances and preferences. Not everyone is going to go work in another country and not everyone is going to be comfortable taking risks all the time. The idea is that we do more of these things as a group and that Canada's economic culture evolves in ways that encourages and supports them. The ideal entrepreneur embodies all the traits while real entrepreneurs exhibit them to varying degrees.

This variance is important to stress when discussing the value of focusing on the top end of the economic value chain because not everyone will be a designer, consultant, international team leader, high tech guru, scientist or educator. Some will have no interest in these careers and some won't have the chance to pursue them either because there are not enough of these jobs to go around or because of other factors. We argue, however, that the *more* we do the things outlined in this book, the *greater* the number of high end jobs available to Canadians. This is good for workers and it is good for the economy.

The new entrepreneur understands this and instinctively seeks out opportunities to move up the value chain rather than get too comfortable further down. So while many businesses and workers will continue to, for example, harvest natural resources and export them or manufacture parts used in more complex products, there will be a new emphasis on not just more value-added activity but the creation of whole new industries based on designing and managing global economic activity.

9) The new Canadian economic entrepreneur has green blood.

More often than not, wealth breeds waste. We have probably all heard stories of penny-pinching billionaires and met wealthy people who dress like they are homeless, but as a society, our wealth has generally meant that we don't have to be efficient or frugal. If the carrots in the fridge are rubbery, we throw them out. If our car is out of style, we buy a new one. Even if only one in ten people read flyers, they are sent to every house. In a million different ways, Canadians waste resources and stress the environment in the name of convenience, luxury or ignorance. This often makes life easier and we are not suggesting a return to a Stone Age lifestyle, but it comes at a cost. This cost, in turn, slows Canada down in the international race for economic success.

The new Canadian entrepreneur fully understands the economic benefits of being green and how greater efficiency, avoiding long-term costs created by compromised ecosystems and a good reputation all add up and provide Canada with a leaner and meaner economy. The new entrepreneur sees that the big picture requires not just lip service to ensuring a healthy environment, but an integrated approach to business that maximizes efficiency while minimizing the drawdown on natural capital and, over time, increasing that natural capital and its ability to underwrite economic activity and quality of life.

The new entrepreneurs may or may not identify themselves as "tree huggers," but they will see a tree's value in terms of preventing soil erosion and providing aesthetic pleasure to talented software designers out for lunch in the park. They will also be careful not to waste wood when using it as an input, and they'll seek out ways to get the most out of natural capital by, for example, investing in green forestry technology. *Waste not, want not* is the mantra of the new Canadian entrepreneur.

10) The new Canadian entrepreneur is a community-builder and networker.

Supporting the arts on a local level is one way that the new Canadian entrepreneur will be actively involved in her community. The list of other ways to help ensure that Canadian society has the vitality needed to support a strong economy is long. Certainly, the new entrepreneur will be a voter, a volunteer, and a collaborator. She will be at the centre of a strong network of relationships and she will seek out interaction with a wide range of diverse people on a regular basis. She will be a global citizen, but she will have strong ties to her local place and be a proud Canadian. She will know instinctively that you have to give to get and that it is people and communities that make for a strong economy, not just profits and growth.

Taking the Leap

There are many factors that will be keys to Canada's economic success in the years ahead. Our argument is that increased focused on six traits—creativity, cosmopolitanism, risk-taking, seeking the top of the value chain, green thinking and social engagement—will rewrite Canada's economic DNA in positive ways and give it the competitive edge and economic outlets it needs to remain prosperous for many more years.

Each trait fosters new ideas and each reinforces the others. Being creative helps Canadians climb the value chain; being social helps Canadians be creative; taking risks and accepting failure requires a strong social support system; green thinking requires innovation; being cosmopolitan enriches Canada's communities; and growing Canada's presence in the knowledge economy depends on all six.

The new Canadian entrepreneur is at once the result of an increased emphasis on cultivating these traits and the embodiment of them. What's important is that the new entrepreneur becomes a part of Canadian society and the Canadian economy. Canada does not need a rare new breed of entrepreneur, but rather a general change across the width and breadth of the Canadian people. Canadians need these traits to seep into their habits and attitudes.

At the end of the day, it will be the development of new ideas that will get the frog to jump out of the pot of water before it boils.

Conclusion

No Frog Legs Please

> "Few will have the greatness to bend history itself; but each of us can work to change a small portion of events, and in the total of all those acts will be written the history of this generation."
> — Robert F. Kennedy

Conservative thinkers will rightly point out that revolutions inevitably lead to the guillotine and gulag—if not literally, then figuratively. By definition, revolutions, and the radical change they bring, upset the status quo. There are winners and losers, there is uncertainty, there is disruption and, sometimes, major problems and unforeseen side-effects erupt. But Canadians don't have the luxury of sticking with the status quo because the world is moving on. The Canadian economy is like an animal that is drinking from a steadily shrinking watering hole. If Canadians don't go find another source of hydration, they are doomed. Turning to our friend the frog in the pot, if the Canadian economy doesn't get out before the water boils, it's in big trouble. It's a choice between revolution or a slow death.

If this is a tad too dramatic, it is at least a choice between major changes or the erosion of Canada's standard of living and the opportunities a dynamic economy brings. Canadians will still be pumping oil, making stuff and showing tourists mountains. But without some fundamental changes to Canada's economic DNA, Canadians will fall behind their competitors and their prospects will decline. In not quite these words, Prime Minister Laurier said that the 20th century would belong to Canada.[107] It is this kind of attitude that is needed *today*.

We realize that the transformations we suggest in this book will upset the Canadian economic apple cart and send shockwaves through some of the more stodgy corners of the Canadian psyche. Business culture has to change in some admittedly major ways. Are CEOs, managers and shareholders ready for a more creative and less predictable workforce? This is a daunting task given that not that long ago women had to wear nylons to work lest businesses couldn't function with bare legs in the office.

Canadians have to be more cosmopolitan and not just in their economic lives. Are Canadians ready to leave the comfort of the familiar? Canada is a wonderfully diverse country but xenophobia and racism are far from things of the past. Canadian kids need to abandon the nest and some will not find their way back. Given that many parents are scared to let their kids walk a few blocks to school, Canadians have a lot of work to do.

Canadians need to take more risks, rely less on traditional manufacturing and resources, pay the upfront costs of green investments and learn to work together in new ways. In the bad old days, the aristocrats would have moaned and groaned about associating with commoners. Today, there will be handwringing about indulging creative types and wasting time on knowledge economy goose chases. Canadians have to step out of their comfort zone—way out of it.

> A great example of Canadian innovation and design stems from Vancouver in the early 1970s. Today, after more than four decades of inspiration, Canadian footwear designer John Fluevog stands tall in a country not known for pushing creative boundaries. His distinctively designed shoes are sold around the world and at Fluevog boutique stores across North America. In many ways Mr. Fluevog encapsulates the themes explored in *The Boiling Frog Dilemma*—how creativity, risk-taking and innovative design are paying off economically and putting Canada at the top of the value chain.

One way or another, change will happen. Canada doesn't have the same economy it had 20 years ago and it won't have the economy it has today 20 years from now. What Canadians can have is some control over how they shape their future economy. History teaches that being reactive is a bad plan. This leaves being proactive. We have suggested a way forward, but there are others to bat around. The point is to avoid just sitting in the pot of water until it's too late. This does not mean that Canadians should pursue every nutty idea that comes along in a wild attempt at initiating change for change's sake. Careful planning, the testing of assumptions, and, yes, even a little conservatism in the form of remembering the lessons of the past are all critical. Nonetheless, if the choices are a continuum with playing roulette on one end and doing nothing but the same old same old on the other end, Canadians clearly need to be leaning toward placing some bets.

We are aware that we don't provide a detailed work plan that Canadians can follow to put the ideas that we have collected in this book into practice. But the general outlines are here: if you are a parent, an educator or a mentor, promote the idea of working abroad for a few years. If you are an employer, figure out ways to harness creative people. If you are developing a business, think internationally first and have your eyes firmly fixed on the top of the value chain. If you are a policymaker, think about how government can facilitate an education system that unleashes creativity and how Canada's institutions can earn back the trust and respect of citizens. If you are an investor, look to the long-term and put your money into transformative ventures. Take big risks. Get to know your neighbour. Don't be afraid of international competition. Find a foreign business partner. We can't tell you exactly how to do each of these things, but we are certain that Canadians can figure it out and that the rewards are worth it.

One of the many metaphors that we played with in our early discussions about this book was derived from an experiment involving some spiders that were sent into space by NASA. The spiders, of course, were used to spinning their webs on earth where a certain amount of gravitational pull was a given. So how did they do in an environment with zero gravity? They bucked the odds and adapted. They found a way to spin webs in a new context.

The lesson we took from this is that you have to have a genetic code that enables you to be flexible and flourish in new and changing circumstances. The spiders did not stop spinning webs. Similarly, Canadians don't have to stop selling natural resources and manufacturing things. But, just as the spiders had to adapt their strengths to a new environment, the Canadian economy has to adapt to a more competitive global economy. We feel that some mucking about with Canada's economic DNA in the ways we describe will prepare Canadians for the new environment.

We have said from the start that government can't do this. It requires small changes on the part of millions of people and businesses. Policymakers and political leaders have a huge role to play—especially in pushing for and allowing the education system to be transformed—but ultimately, it is up to the small business owner, the young entrepreneur, the CEO, the parent, the ticket buyer, the person with an idea, and so on, to embrace the vision of a more creative, more social, more fearless, more efficient and more cosmopolitan economy.

We have also said from the beginning that these ideas are not new. They have been kicking around in various forms for years. What's new is seeing them as a unit—a matching set—and moving forward on them together. A creative society that is not also a gregarious and cosmopolitan society won't get the job done. Taking more risks without moving up the value chain and getting greener is not sufficient. Canada needs change on all six fronts. At the same time, it has to be on a large scale. An extra fine arts program here, a few extra kids working overseas there and so on will not produce the results Canada needs. You name the cliché—go big or go home, big rewards require big risks, all or nothing—they all apply.

The booms and busts of being a commodities supplier, the unmistakable shift in manufacturing, Canada's odd invisibility, the rise of opportunities in the creative economy, the pressure to adopt greener practices, the paralyzing effects of fear, and the clear advantages of networking at home and abroad are the reality Canadians face. These are hard things to dispute. Some are heating the water under our frog friend and some offer ways out of the pot.

Admittedly, the six genetic mutations that we argue will create a new Canadian entrepreneur who, if sufficiently present throughout the economy, will give Canada the edge it needs to flourish in the global economy are not the only way out of the pot of hot water. Hence, we end with this challenge: if you see other ways for Canadians to forge a bright economic future—either in addition to, or instead of, the six things we suggest—give voice to them. Tell your neighbour, your boss, your co-workers, your employees, your MP, your kids. We can't *just* talk about it, but the more we do, the more likely it is that change will happen.

Endnotes

[1] Robert Roach. 2010. *State of the West 2010: Western Canadian Demographic and Economic Trends*. Figures 1, 24, 101 and 108.

[2] "… economic activity is increasingly being organized on a global basis. New and more aggressive competitors are emerging, and new technologies are reshaping entire industries." Competition Policy Review Panel. 2008. *Compete to Win. Final Report.*

[3] State of the Union Address 2011. http://www.whitehouse.gov/the-press-office/2011/01/25/remarks-president-state-union-address

[4] See Francis Fukuyama. 1995. *Trust: The Social Virtues and the Creation of Prosperity.*

[5] Roger Martin and Richard Florida. 2009. *Ontario in the Creative Age*. Martin Prosperity Institute.

[6] Andrew Potter. 2009. "What would you pay for a map with no roads?" *Maclean's.* February 19.

[7] Email correspondence, July 14, 2011.

[8] *Ibid.*

[9] Philip Cross. 2011. "Recent Trends in Business Investment." *Canadian Economic Observer.* March. Statistics Canada.

[10] Wall Street Journal. 2009. "Cutting the Gordonian Knot: Nostalgia for a pre-post-industrial Britain won't solve the U.K.'s economic problems." October 7.

[11] BBC News. 2011. "New JCB jobs during Osborne visit." February 10.

[12] Shantha Shanmugalingam, Ruth Puttick and Stian Westlake. 2010. *Rebalancing Act.* National Endowment for Science, Technology and the Arts.

[13] *Ibid.*

[14] *Ibid.*

[15] Potash, uranium and nickel are notable exceptions in which Canada is a significant—if not dominant—global producer.

[16] PricewaterhouseCoopers. 2009. *Rebuilding the Global Economy.*

[17] Irwin Steltzer. 2010. "The butterfly effect and world economics." BBC World Service.

[18] International Monetary Fund eLibrary Data http://elibrary-data.imf.org/DataReport.aspx?c=1449299&d=33061&e=170921.

[19] Premier's Council for Economic Strategy. 2011. *Shaping Alberta's Future.*

20. Globe and Mail. 2010. "Canadian companies: know your competitors before going global." November 10.
21. http://www.forbes.com/lists/2011/6/best-countries-11_land.html
22. United Nations Development Program Human Development Index 2010 http://hdr.undp.org/en/statistics/
23. Klaus Schwab. 2010. *Global Competitiveness Report 2010-11.* World Economic Forum.
24. Mercer Quality of Living Worldwide City rRankings 2010 http://www.mercer.com/press-releases/quality-of-living-report-2010
25. The Economist. 2011. "Where the livin' is easiest." February 21.
26. Monocle Magazine. 2011. *Special Edition: The Liveable Cities Index.* July/August.
27. Knight Frank LLP. 2011. *The Wealth Report: A Global Perspective on Prime Property and Wealth 2011.*
28. George W. Bush in a speech to Joint Session of Congress, September 20, 2001. http://www.historyplace.com/speeches/gw-bush-9-11.htm
29. Translation of speech by Osama Bin Laden broadcast on Arabic television channel al-Jazeera, November 12, 2002. BBC News World Edition http://news.bbc.co.uk/2/hi/middle_east/2455845.stm
30. http://www.euromoney.com/Article/2297318/Category/17/ChannelPage/10690/Finance-minister-of-the-year-Jim-Flaherty-Canada.html
31. http://www.time.com/time/specials/packages/article/0,28804,1972075_1972078_1972505,00.html
32. Faiz Jamil. 2011."India's knowledge of Canada limited to Russell Peters." CBC News online. June 22. http://www.cbc.ca/news/world/story/2011/06/21/f-vp-jamil.html
33. Sean Fine. 2010. "New Canadians need Old World links." *The Globe and Mail.* December 16.
34. Deloitte Canada. 2001. "The Future of Productivity: An Eight-Step Game Plan for Canada."
35. http://www.ted.com/talks/ken_robinson_says_schools_kill_creativity.html
36. http://www.econlib.org/library/Enc1/EconomicGrowth.html
37. Roger Martin and Richard Florida. 2009. *Ontario in the Creative Age.* Martin Prosperity Institute.
38. Murray Campbell. 2009. "McGuinty would be wise to focus on the wounded." *Globe and Mail.* February 7.
39. http://www.creativityatwork.com/articlesContent/whatis.htm
40. Rollo May. 2007. "The Courage to Create." *Journal of Humanistic Psychology.* January: 47.
41. R. J. Sternberg and T. I. Lubart. 1995. *Defying the Crowd: Cultivating Creativity in a Culture of Conformity.*
42. Paul Romer. No date. "Economic Growth." *The Concise Encyclopedia of Economics.* http://www.econlib.org/library/Enc/EconomicGrowth.html
43. *Ibid.*
44. Ken Robinson. 2001. *Out of Our Minds: Learning to be Creative.*
45. www.oecd.org/edu/pisa/2009
46. Daniel Pink. 2006. *A Whole New Mind. Why Right-Brainers Will Rule the Future.*
47. Ken Robinson. 2001. *Out of Our Minds: Learning to be Creative.*
48. *Ibid.*
49. *Ibid.*
50. http://gapingvoid.com/2004/07/25/how-to-be-creative/
51. New York Times. 2010. "Discovering the Virtues of a Wandering Mind." June 28.
52. Gregory Berns. 2008. *Iconoclast: A Neuroscientist Reveals How to Think Differently.*
53. Globe and Mail. 2011. "Give Canada's visiting brains a boost." July 10.
54. Excerpt from Startup Visa Canada website www.startupvisa.ca.

[55] Globe and Mail. 2011. "Immigrant tech stars face hurdles in quest to start business in Canada." July 8.

[56] Ibid.

[57] Martha Piper. 2007. "The Butterfly Effect: Transforming Alberta's Post-Secondary Institutions" in Robert Roach, ed. *Alberta's Energy Legacy: Ideas for the Future*. Canada West Foundation.

[58] Sean Fine. 2010. "New Canadians need Old World links." *The Globe and Mail*. December 16.

[59] Andrea Mandel-Campbell. 2007. *Why Mexicans Don't Drink Molson*.

[60] Eric Reguly. 2011. "Gimme, Gimme, Gimme." *Report on Business Magazine*. July/August.

[61] Ibid.

[62] Email correspondence, August 2011.

[63] Greg Linden, Kenneth L. Kraemer and Jason Dedrick. 2009. "Who Captures Value in a Global Innovation Network? The Case of Apple's iPod." *Communications of the ACM*. March, 52:3.

[64] Greg Linden, Jason Dedrick and Ken Kraemer. 2009. "Innovation and Job Creation in a Global Economy: The Case of Apple's iPod." Industry Studies Association 2009 Annual Conference.

[65] US Bureau of Labor Statistics, accessed June 2011 http://www.bls.gov/lau/

[66] Globe and Mail. 2011. "Remade in Canada: the Future of Factories." June. http://investdb1.theglobeandmail.com/servlet/story/GAM.20110616.RBB2QANDA0616ATL/GIStory/

[67] Email correspondence, July 14, 2011.

[68] Barrie McKenna. 2011. "For Canadian manufacturers, foreign assets tantalizingly cheap." *Globe and Mail*. June 13. http://m.theglobeandmail.com/report-on-business/economy/manufacturing/for-canadian-manufacturers-foreign-assets-tantalizingly-cheap/article2057614/?service=mobile

[69] Malcolm Gladwell. 2011. "Creation Myth: Xerox PARC, Apple, and the truth about innovation." *The New Yorker Magazine*. May 16.

[70] Comments given at the Cannes Lions International Advertising Festival cited in *The Globe and Mail*, June 20, 2011 ("Gladwell touts benefits of developing products late").

[71] Email correspondence, August 2011.

[72] Deloitte Canada. 2001. "The Future of Productivity: An Eight-Step Game Plan for Canada."

[73] Institute for Competitiveness and Prosperity. 2003. "Striking Similarities: Attitudes and Ontario's Prosperity Gap." *Working Paper 4*.

[74] Deloitte Canada. 2001. "The Future of Productivity: An Eight-Step Game Plan for Canada."

[75] Ibid.

[76] Andy Hoffman and Elizabeth Church. 2006. "Munk Rants: Where's Miners' Courage?" *Globe and Mail*. September 13.

[77] Andrea Mandel-Campbell. 2007. *Why Mexicans Don't Drink Molson*.

[78] Franklin D. Roosevelt, Inaugural Address, March 4, 1933, as published in Samuel Rosenman (ed.). *The Public Papers of Franklin D. Roosevelt, Volume Two: The Year of Crisis, 1933*. Retrieved from http://historymatters.gmu.edu/d/5057/

[79] For an excellent description of the mechanics of fear in the brain, see Chapter 2 of Steven Johnston. 2004. *Mind Wide Open: Your Brain and the Neuroscience of Everyday Life*.

[80] Steven Johnson. 2004. *Mind Wide Open: Your Brain and the Neuroscience of Everyday Life*.

[81] Alina Tugend on CBC Radio's "The Current." May 18, 2011.

[82] Tim Hartford. 2011. *Adapt: Why Success Always Starts with Failure*.

[83] S. Asch. 1951. "Effects of Group Pressure upon the Modification and Distortion of Judgments" in H.S. Guetzkow (ed.). *Groups, Leadership and Men: Research in Human Relations*.

[84] Patrick Finn. Email interview June 11, 2011.

[85] Tim Hartford on CBC Radio's "The Current." May 18, 2011.

[86] Daniel Isenberg. 2011. "Entrepreneurs and The Cult of Failure." *Harvard Business Review*. 89:4.

[87] Henry Ford. 1923. "My Life and Work." Cited in Gregory Berns. 2010. *Iconoclast: A Neuroscientist Reveals how to Think Differently.*

[88] Paul Hawken. 2005. *The Ecology of Commerce.*

[89] Lester R. Brown. 2001. *Eco-Economy: Building and Economy for the Earth.* Earth Policy Institute.

[90] US Department of Commerce. 2010. *Measuring the Green Economy.*

[91] Globe Foundation. 2010. *British Columbia's Green Economy: Building a Strong Low-Carbon Future.*

[92] Green Economy Initiative. http://www.unep.org/greeneconomy/AboutGEI/tabid/1370/Default.aspx

[93] Russell Mitchell Group. 2010. T*he 2010 SDTC Cleantech Growth and Go-To-Market Report.*

[94] Green Economy Initiative. 2010. *The Green Economy Report Brochure.*

[95] Eco Canada. 2010. *Defining the Green Economy.*

[96] Email correspondence, August 2011.

[97] Robert Roach and Shawna Ritchie. 2011. *The Green Grail: Economic Diversification and the Green Economy in Western Canada.* Canada West Foundation.

[98] US Department of Commerce. 2010. *Measuring the Green Economy.*

[99] Adam M. Grant and James W. Berry. 2011. "The Necessity of Others in the Mother of Invention: Intrinsic and Prosocial Motivations, Perspective Taking, and Creativity. *Academy of Management Journal.* 54:1.

[100] Robert Putnam. 1993. *Making Democracy Work: Civic Traditions in Modern Italy.*

[101] "But even if political association did not directly contribute to the progress of civil association, to destroy the former would be to impair the latter. When citizens can only meet in public for certain purposes, they regard such meetings as a strange proceeding of rare occurrence, and they rarely think at all about it. When they are allowed to meet freely for all purposes, they ultimately look upon public association as the universal, or in a manner the sole means, which men can employ to accomplish the different purposes they may have in view. Every new want instantly revives the notion. The art of association then becomes, as I have said before, the mother of action, studied and applied by all." Alexis de Tocqueville. *Democracy In America.* Book 2, Chapter 5. "Of The Use Which The Americans Make Of Public Associations In Civil Life."

[102] Adam M. Grant and James W. Berry. 2011. "The Necessity of Others in the Mother of Invention: Intrinsic and Prosocial Motivations, Perspective Taking, and Creativity. *Academy of Management Journal.* 54:1.

[103] Francis Fukuyama. 1995. *Trust: The Social Virtues and the Creation of Prosperity.*

[104] Ibid. Page 356. Fukuyama borrows Putnam's definition of social capital: "features of social organization, such as trust, norms, and networks, that can improve the efficiency of society by facilitating coordinated actions." Robert Putnam. 1993. *Making Democracy Work: Civic Traditions in Modern Italy.*

[105] Richard Florida. 2002. *The Rise of the Creative Class.*

[106] Greg Ip. 2010. *The Little Book of Economics: How the Economy Works in the Real World.*

[107] What he actually said was: "Canada has been modest in its history, although its history is heroic in many ways. But its history, in my estimation, is only commencing. It is commencing in this century. The 19th century was the century of the United States. I think we can claim that it is Canada that shall fill the 20th century."– Prime Minister Wilfrid Laurier, in a speech to the Canadian Club of Ottawa, 18 January 1904. He said essentially the same thing on October 14, 1904 at Massey Hall: "I tell you that the 19th century has been the United States' development. The past 100 years has been filled with the pages of their history. Let me tell you, my fellow countrymen, that all the signs point this way, that the 20th century shall be the century of Canada and of Canadian development. For the next 17 years, nay for the next 100, Canada shall be the star toward which all men who love progress and freedom shall come."

Bibliography

Asch, S. 1951. "Effects of Group Pressure upon the Modification and Distortion of Judgments" in H.S. Guetzkow (ed.). *Groups, Leadership and Men: Research in Human Relations.*

Ali, Roxanne and Yves Poisson. 2007. *Economic Transformation North of 60°: Outcomes Report.* Public Policy Forum.

Atkinson, Robert D. and Scott M. Andes. 2009. *The Atlantic Century: Benchmarking EU and U.S. Innovation and Competitiveness.* The Information Technology and Innovation Foundation.

Bayoumi, Tamim, Vladimir Klyuev, and Martin Mühleisen (eds). 2007. *Northern Star: Canada's Path to Economic Prosperity.* Occasional paper 258. International Monetary Fund.

BBC News. "New JCB jobs during Osborne visit." February 10, 2011.

BC Competition Council. 2006. *Enhancing the Competitiveness of British Columbia.* Government of British Columbia.

Beatley, Timothy. 2000. *Green Uranism: Learning from European Cities.*

Beinhocker, Eric D. 2006. *The Origin of Wealth.*

Bennett, Joe. 2008. *Where Underpants Come From: From Checkout to Cotton Field – Travels Through the New China.*

Berger, Warren. 2009. *Glimmer: How Design Can Transform Your Life, Business, and Maybe Even the World.*

Berkun, Scott. 2010. *The Myths of Innovation.*

Berns, Gregory. 2010. *Iconoclast: A Neuroscientist Reveals How to Think Differently.*

Boland Jr., Richard J. and Fred Collopy (eds). 2004. Managing as Designing.

Brenner, Reuven and Gabrielle A. Brenner. 2007. "How to Attract, Groom and Retain Talent in Canada." *Research Paper Summary.* Competition Policy Review Panel.

Brown, Lester R. 2001. *Eco-Economy: Building and Economy for the Earth.* Earth Policy Institute.

California Community Colleges. 2009. "Understand the Green Economy in California."

Campbell, Murray. 2009. "McGuinty would be wise to focus on the wounded." *Globe and Mail,* February 7.

Canada West Foundation. 1987. "Economic Development and Diversification in Western Canada."

Canada25. 2001. *A New Magnetic North: How Canada Can Attract and Retain Young Talent.* Canada25.

Canadian Council of Chief Executives. 2006. *From Bronze To Gold: A Blueprint for Canadian Leadership in a Transforming World.*

Carlson, Lance. 2007. "Alberta by Design: The Creativity and Innovation Equation" in *Alberta's Energy Legacy: Ideas for the Future.* Robert Roach (ed.). Canada West Foundation.

Chamberlain, Lisa. 2008. *Slackonomics: Generation X in the Age of Creative Destruction.*

Chambers, Edward J. and Chris Ryan. 2009. "Breaking the Boom and Bust: Exploring Thirty Years of Diversification in Western Canada." *Information Bulletin* 121. Western Centre for Economic Research.

Chambers, Edward J. and Mike Percy. 1992. *Western Canada in the International Economy.*

Collier, Paul. 2010. *The Plundered Planet: Why We Must—and How We Can—Manage Nature for Global Prosperity.*

Collins, Jim. 2001. *Good to Great: Why Some Companies Make the Leap...and Others Don't.*

Competition Policy Review Panel. 2007. *Sharpening Canada's Competitive Edge.* Government of Canada.

Competition Policy Review Panel. 2008. *Compete to Win: Final Report.* Government of Canada.

Conference Board of Canada. 2002. *Canada 2010: Challenges and Choices at Home and Abroad.*

Conference Board of Canada. 2003. *Defining the Canadian Advantage.*

Conference Board of Canada. 2004. *Exploring Canada's Innovation Character: Benchmarking Against Global Best.*

Conference Board of Canada. 2004. *How Can Canada Prosper in Tomorrow's World?*

Conference Board of Canada. 2005. *Performance and Potential 2005-06 – The World and Canada: Trends Reshaping Our Future.*

Conference Board of Canada. 2007. *Mission Possible Executive Summary: Sustainable Prosperity for Canada.*

Conference Board of Canada. 2008. *The Canada Project Progress Report 2007: The Roads Not Travelled.*

Côté, André and Poisson Yves. 2007. *Improving Canada's Business Environment and Competitiveness: Outcomes Report.* Public Policy Forum.

Courchene, Thomas J. 2007. "Global Futures for Canada's Global Cities." *Policy Matters,* 8(2). The Institute of Research on Public Policy.

Cross, Philip. 2011."Recent Trends in Business Investment." *Canadian Economic Observer.* March. Statistics Canada.

Cunningham, Storm. 2008. *reWealth: Stake Your Claim in the $2 Trillion reDevelopment Trend That's Renewing the World.*

D'Aquino, Thomas Paul and David Stewart-Patterson. 2001. *Northern Edge: How Canadians Can Triumph in the Global Economy.*

Das, Satya. 2009. *Green Oil.*

Deloitte Canada. 2001. "The Future of Productivity: An Eight-Step Game Plan for Canada."

den Butter, F.A.G., J.L. Mohlmann, and P. Wit. 2008. "Trade and product innovations as sources for productivity increases: an empirical analysis." *Journal of Productivity Analysis,* 30, 210-211.

Diers, Jim. 2004. *Neighbor Power: Building Community the Seattle Way.*

Duruflé, Gilles. 2009. *Why Venture Capital is Essential to the Canadian Economy: The Impact of Venture Capital on the Canadian Economy.* Canada's Venture Capital and Private Equity Association (CVCA).

Dutton, Denis. 2009. *The Art Instinct: Beauty, Pleasure, and Human Evolution.*

Eco Canada. 2010. *Defining the Green Economy.*

Economic Council of Canada. 1984. *Western Transitions.*

The Economist. 2011. "Where the livin' is easiest." February 21.

Elkus Jr., Richard J. 2008. *Winner Take All: How Competitiveness Shapes the Fate of Nations.*

Fine, Sean. 2010. "New Canadians need Old World links." *The Globe and Mail.* December 16.

Florida, Richard. 2002. *The Rise of the Creative Class: And How It's Transforming Work, Leisure, Community and Everyday Life.*

Florida, Richard. 2008. *Who's Your City?: How the Creative Economy is Making Where to Live The Most Important Decision of Your Life.*

Friedman, Thomas L. 2000. *The Lexus and the Olive Tree: Understanding Globalization.*

Friedman, Thomas L. 2006. *The World is Flat: A Brief History of the Twenty-First Century, Updated and Expanded.*

Fukuyama, Francis. 1995. *Trust: The Social Virtues and the Creation of Prosperity.*

Gardner, Dan. 2009. *Risk: Why We Fear the Things We Shouldn't – and Put Ourselves in Greater Danger.*

Gibbins, Roger and Robert Roach. 2009. *Playing for Keeps: Boosting Western Canada's Economic Competitiveness in the Post-Recession World.*

Gibbins, Roger. 2010. *An Extraordinary Future: A Strategic Vision for Western Canada.* Canada West Foundation.

Gladwell, Malcolm. "Creation Myth: Xerox PARC, Apple, and the truth about innovation." *The New Yorker Magazine.* May 16.

Global Insight. 2008. *U.S. Metro Economies: GMP – The Engines of America's Growth.*

Globe Foundation. 2010a. *British Columbia's Green Economy: Building a Strong Low-Carbon Future.*

Globe Foundation. 2010b. "British Columbia's Green Economy: Project Methodology."

Globe and Mail. 2010. "Canadian companies: know your competitors before going global." November 10.

Globe and Mail. 2011. "Give Canada's visiting brains a boost." July 10.

Globe and Mail. 2011. "Immigrant tech stars face hurdles in quest to start business in Canada." July 8.

Grant, Adam M. and James W. Berry. 2011. "The Necessity of Others in the Mother of Invention: Intrinsic and Prosocial Motivations, Perspective Taking, and Creativity. *Academy of Management Journal.* 54:1.

Green Economy Initiative. 2010a. Website. http://www.unep.org/greeneconomy/AboutGEI/tabid/1370/Default.aspx

Green Economy Initiative. 2010b. *The Green Economy Report Brochure.*

Gruending, Dennis (ed). 2004. *Great Canadian Speeches.*

Hart, Michael. 2002. *A Trading Nation: Canadian Trade Policy From Colonialism to Globalization.*

Hartford, Tim. 2011. *Adapt: Why Success Always Starts with Failure.*

Harvard Business Essentials. 2003. *Managing Creativity and Innovation.*

Hawken, Paul, Amory Lovins, and L. Hunter Lovins. 1999. *Natural Capitalism: Creating the Next Industrial Revolution.*

Hawken, Paul. 2005. *The Ecology of Commerce: A Declaration of Sustainability.*

Heintzman, Andrew. 2010. *The New Entrepreneurs: Building a Green Economy for the Future.*

Hirsch, Todd. 2006. *Coming Up NEXT: The Transformation of Western Canada's Economy.* Canada West Foundation.

Hirsch, Todd. 2006. *Shaping Our Future: Creative Ideas for Transforming Western Canada's Economy.* The NEXT West Project. Canada West Foundation.

Hodgson, Glen and Anne Park Shannon. 2007. *Mission Possible: Stellar Canadian Performance in the Global Economy.* The Canada Project. Conference Board of Canada.

Hoffman, Andy and Elizabeth Church. 2006. "Munk Rants: Where's Miners' Courage?" *Globe and Mail.* September 13.

Hollender, Jeffrey and Bill Breen. 2010. *The Responsibility Revolution: How the Next Generation of Businesses Will Win.*

Ingram, Jay. 2008. *The Daily Planet Book of Cool Ideas: Global Warming and What People are Doing About It.*

Innovas. 2009. *Low Carbon and Environmental Goods and Services: An Industry Analysis.*

Institute for Competitiveness and Prosperity. 2003. "Striking Similarities: Attitudes and Ontario's Prosperity Gap." Working Paper 4.

Ip, Greg. 2010. *The Little Book of Economics: How the Economy Works in the Real World.*

Isenberg, Daniel. 2011. "Entrepreneurs and The Cult of Failure." *Harvard Business Review.* April.

Jacobs, Jane. 1970. *The Economy of Cities.*

Jamil, Faiz. 2011."India's knowledge of Canada limited to Russell Peters." CBC News online. June 22.

Johnson, Steven. 2004. *Mind Wide Open: Your Brain and the Neuroscience of Everyday Life.*

Kao, John. 2007. *Innovation Nation: How America Is Losing Its Innovation Edge, Why It Matters, and What We Can Do to Get It Back.*

Kelly, Tom and Jonathan Littman. 2005. *The Ten Faces of Innovation.*

Knight Frank LLP. 2011. *The Wealth Report: A Global Perspective on Prime Property and Wealth 2011.*

Linden, Greg, Jason Dedrick and Ken Kraemer. 2009. "Innovation and Job Creation in a Global Economy: The Case of Apple's iPod." Industry Studies Association 2009 Annual Conference.

Linden, Greg, Kenneth L. Kraemer and Jason Dedrick. 2009. "Who Captures Value in a Global Innovation Network? The Case of Apple's iPod." *Communications of the ACM.* March, 52:3.

Lucas, R. 1988. "On the Mechanics of Economic Development." *Journal of Monetary Economics,* 22, 3–42.

Mandel-Campbell, Andrea. 2007. *Why Mexicans Don't Drink Molson.*

Mansell, Robert and Mike Percy. 1990. *Strength in Adversity: A Study of the Alberta Economy.*

Marck, Paul. 2010. "We've Come a Long Way, Baby." *Alberta Venture.* August 2010.

Martin, Roger. 2007. *The Opposable Mind*.

Martin, Roger and Richard Florida. 2009. *Ontario in the Creative Age*. Martin Prosperity Institute.

Martin, Roger and James Milway. 2007. "Assessing the Potential Impact of a National Champions Policy on Canada's Competitiveness." *Research Paper Summary*. Competition Policy Review Panel. Government of Canada.

Martin, Roger L. and Michael E. Porter. 2001. "Canadian Competitiveness: A Decade after the Crossroads."

Milner, Henry. 2002. *Civic Literacy: How Informed Citizens Make Democracy Work*.

Monocle Magazine. 2011. *Special Edition: The Liveable Cities Index*. July/August.

Nadeau, Robert L. 2002. The Wealth of Nature: *How Mainstream Economics Has Failed the Environment*.

Nussbaum, Martha C. 2010. *Not For Profit: Why Democracy Needs the Humanities*.

Orrell, David. 2010. Economyths: *Ten Ways Economics Gets it Wrong*.

PEW Charitable Trusts. 2009. "The Clean Energy Economy: Repowering Jobs, Businesses and Investments Across America."

Phyper, John-David and Paul MacLean. 2009. *Good to Green: Managing Business Risks and Opportunities in the Age of Environmental Awareness*.

Pink, Daniel. 2006. *A Whole New Mind. Why Right-Brainers Will Rule the Future*.

Piper, Martha. 2007. "The Butterfly Effect: Transforming Alberta's Post-Secondary Education System" in *Alberta's Energy Legacy: Ideas for the Future*. Robert Roach (ed.). Canada West Foundation.

Porter, Michael E. 1998. "Clusters and the New Economics of Competition." *Harvard Business Review*.

Porter, Michael E. 2003. "The Economic Performance of Regions." *Regional Studies*, 37(6&7), 549-578.

Porter, Michael E. and Klaus Schwab. 2008. *The Global Competitiveness Report 2008-2009*. World Economic Forum.

Porter, Michael E., Xavier Sala-i-Martin, and Klaus Schwab. 2007. *The Global Competitiveness Report 2007-2008*. World Economic Forum.

Potter, Andrew. 2009. "What would you pay for a map with no roads?" *Maclean's*. February 19.

Premier's Council for Economic Strategy. 2011. *Shaping Alberta's Future*.

PricewaterhouseCoopers. 2009. *Rebuilding the Global Economy*.

Putnam, Robert D. 1993. *Making Democracy Work: Civic Traditions in Modern Italy*.

Putnam, Robert D. 2000. *Bowling Alone: The Collapse and Revival of American Community*.

Rauch, Jonathan. 2001. "The New Old Economy: Oil, Computers, and the Reinvention of the Earth." *The Atlantic Monthly,* January.

Rechelbacher, Horst M. 2008. *Minding Your Business: Profits that Restore the Planet*.

Reguly, Eric. 2011. "Gimme, Gimme, Gimme." *Report on Business Magazine*. July/August.

Reinert, Erik S. 2007. *How Rich Countries Got Rich...and Why Poor Countries Stay Poor*.

Rhéaume, Gilles and John Roberts. 2007. *Mission Possible: A Canadian Resources Strategy for the Boom and Beyond*. The Canada Project. Conference Board of Canada.

Ridley, Matt. 2010. *The Rational Optimist: How Prosperity Evolves*.

Rifkin, Jeremy. 1995. *The End of Work: The Decline of the Global Labor Force and the Dawn of the Post-Market Era*.

Robert Roach. 2010. *State of the West 2010: Western Canadian Demographic and Economic Trends*. Canada West Foundation.

Robinson, Ken. 2001. *Out of Our Minds: Learning to Be Creative*.

Robinson, Ken and Lou Aronica. 2009. *The Element.: How Finding Your Passion Changes Everything*.

Romer, Paul. 1986. "Increasing Returns and Long Run Growth." *Journal of Political Economy*, 94.

Romer, Paul. No date. "Economic Growth." *The Concise Encyclopedia of Economics*. http://www.econlib.org/library/Enc/EconomicGrowth.html

May, Rollo. 2007. "The Courage to Create." *Journal of Humanistic Psychology*. January: 47.

Rosenberg, N. 2004. *Innovation and Economic Growth.* Organisation for Economic Co-operation and Development.

Rowlands, Dane. 2007. "Formal and Informal Barriers to Canadian FDI." *Research Paper Summary.* Competition Policy Review Panel. Government of Canada.

Royal Commission on the Economic Union and Development Prospects for Canada. 1985. *Report, Volumes 1-3.*

Rubin, Jeff. 2009. *Why Your World is About to Get a Whole Lot Smaller.*

Rugman, Alan and Jing Li. 2007. "Are There Global or Regional Supply Chains? Implications for Head Office Location in Canada." *Research Paper Summary.* Competition Policy Review Panel. Government of Canada.

Russell Mitchell Group. 2010. *The 2010 SDTC Cleantech Growth and Go-To-Market Report.*

Samarasekera, Indira. 2007. "Investing in Talent: The Gift that Sustains Transformation." Philanthropic Foundations Conference 2007.

San, Chan Sau. 2006. "Rationales and Options for Diversification in Macao." Monetary Authority of Macao.

Schwab, Klaus. 2010. *Global Competitiveness Report 2010-11.* World Economic Forum.

Schor, Juliet B. 2010. *Plenitude: The New Economics of True Wealth.*

Schwartz, Peter. 1996. *The Art of the Long View: Planning for the Future in an Uncertain World.*

Senor, Dan and Saul Singer. 2009. *Start-Up Nation: The Story of Israel's Economic Miracle.*

Steltzer, Irwin. 2010. "The butterfly effect and world economics." BBC World Service.

Shantha Shanmugalingam, Ruth Puttick and Stian Westlake. 2010. *Rebalancing Act.* National Endowment for Science, Technology and the Arts.

Sharpe, Andrew and Meghna Banerjee. 2007. "Assessing Canada's Ability to Compete for Foreign Direct Investment." *Research Paper Summary.* Competition Policy Review Panel. Government of Canada.

Soete, L. 2007. "From Industrial to Innovation Policy." *Journal of Industry, Competition and Trade,* 7.

Sternberg, R. J. and T. I. Lubart. 1995. *Defying the Crowd: Cultivating Creativity in a Culture of Conformity.*

Tapscott, Don and Anthony D. Williams. 2006. *Wikinomics: How Mass Collaboration Changes Everything.*

Tertzakian, Peter and Ketih Hollihan. 2009. *The End of Energy Obesity: Breaking Today's Energy Addiction for a Prosperous and Secure Tomorrow.*

US Department of Commerce. 2010. *Measuring the Green Economy.*

Vietor, Richard H. K. 2007. *How Countries Compete: Strategy, Structure, and Government in the Global Economy.*

Wall Street Journal. "Cutting the Gordonian Knot: Nostalgia for a pre-post-industrial Britain won't solve the U.K.'s economic problems." October 7, 2009.

Wentzell, Corey. 2010. "White Paper on Economic Diversification (Draft)." Edmonton Chamber of Commerce.

Zakaria, Fareed. 2008. *The Post-American World.*

Author Biographies

Todd Hirsch received his BA Honors in Economics from the University of Alberta and MA in Economics from the University of Calgary. Since completing his post-secondary education in 1993, he has held a series of economist positions at a variety of for-profit, nonprofit and public sector organizations, including the Canada West Foundation, Canadian Pacific Railway and the Bank of Canada.

Todd joined ATB Financial in May 2007 as Senior Economist where he provides economic information and intelligence to the various lines of business at ATB. He also tracks current economic developments and spends much of his time as a public speaker to both internal and external audiences.

Todd provides economic commentary to numerous TV and radio shows and is a frequent contributor to newspapers such as the *Globe and Mail* and the *Calgary Herald*. He also teaches a course in Economics at the University of Calgary, serves as a mentor for the Economics Society of Calgary's Student Mentorship Program and is the Chair of the Board of Directors of the Calgary Arts Academy. Born in Edmonton, Todd has been based in Calgary since 1989.

Robert Roach has a BA and MA in Political Science from the University of Calgary. Robert is the Vice President, Research at the Canada West Foundation. He started at the Foundation in 1995 and has worked on a broad array of public policy topics including economic development, local government, demographic trends, the nonprofit sector, public opinion, regional cooperation, environmental policy, democratic reform and public finance.

Robert has been President of the Economics Society of Calgary, is a Course Director and Instructor in the Faculty of Extension at the University of Alberta and is the Vice Chair of the Calgary Arts Academy. Born in Edmonton, Robert has called Calgary home since 1974.